Classroom Assessment Essentials

ASCD MEMBER BOOK

Many ASCD members received this book as a
member benefit upon its initial release.

Learn more at: **www.ascd.org/memberbooks**

Also by Susan M. Brookhart

How to Look at Student Work to Uncover Student Thinking

*Advancing Formative Assessment in Every Classroom:
A Guide for Instructional Leaders*, 2nd Edition

What We Know About Grading: What Works, What Doesn't, and What's Next

How to Use Grading to Improve Learning

How to Give Effective Feedback to Your Students, 2nd Edition

How to Make Decisions with Different Kinds of Student Assessment Data

*Formative Classroom Walkthroughs: How Principals and
Teachers Collaborate to Raise Student Achievement*

How to Design Questions and Tasks to Assess Student Thinking

*Grading and Group Work: How Do I Assess Individual
Learning When Students Work Together?*

How to Create and Use Rubrics for Formative Assessment and Grading

Learning Targets: Helping Students Aim for Understanding in Today's Lesson

How to Assess Higher-Order Thinking Skills in Your Classroom

The Formative Assessment Learning Cycle (Quick Reference Guide)

Grading for Student Learning (Quick Reference Guide)

Rubrics for Formative Assessment and Grading (Quick Reference Guide)

Giving Students Effective Feedback (Quick Reference Guide)

Classroom Assessment Essentials

SUSAN M. BROOKHART

 ascd

Arlington, Virginia USA

2800 Shirlington Road, Suite 1001 • Arlington, VA 22206 USA
Phone: 800-933-2723 or 703-578-9600 • Fax: 703-575-5400
Website: www.ascd.org • Email: member@ascd.org
Author guidelines: www.ascd.org/write

Richard Culatta, *Chief Executive Officer;* Anthony Rebora, *Chief Content Officer;* Genny Ostertag, *Managing Director, Book Acquisitions & Editing;* Mary Beth Nielsen, *Director, Book Editing;* Liz Wegner, *Editor;* Thomas Lytle, *Creative Director;* Donald Ely, *Art Director;* Daniela Aguero/The Hatcher Group, *Graphic Designer;* Cynthia Stock, *Typesetter;* Kelly Marshall, *Production Manager;* Shajuan Martin, *E-Publishing Specialist*

All web links in this book are correct as of the publication date below but may have become inactive or otherwise modified since that time. If you notice a deactivated or changed link, please email books@ascd.org with the words "Link Update" in the subject line. In your message, please specify the web link, the book title, and the page number on which the link appears.

PAPERBACK ISBN: 978-1-4166-3252-8   ASCD product #124001
PDF EBOOK ISBN: 978-1-4166-3253-5; see Books in Print for other formats.
Quantity discounts are available: email programteam@ascd.org or call 800-933-2723, ext. 5773, or 703-575-5773. For desk copies, go to www.ascd.org/deskcopy.

ASCD Member Book No. FY23-11 (Nov 2023 PSI+). ASCD Member Books mail to Premium (P), Select (S), and Institutional Plus (I+) members on this schedule: Jan, PSI+; Feb, P; Apr, PSI+; May, P; Jul, PSI+; Aug, P; Sep, PSI+; Nov, PSI+; Dec, P. For current details on membership, see www.ascd.org/membership.

Library of Congress Cataloging-in-Publication Data
Names: Brookhart, Susan M., author.
Title: Classroom assessment essentials / Susan M. Brookhart.
Description: Arlington, VA USA : ASCD, [2024] | Includes bibliographical
    references and index.
Identifiers: LCCN 2023026198 (print) | LCCN 2023026199 (ebook) | ISBN
    9781416632528 (paperback) | ISBN 9781416632535 (pdf)
Subjects: LCSH: Educational evaluation. | Educational tests and
    measurements—Evaluation. | Classroom environment—Social aspects. |
    Teacher effectiveness.
Classification: LCC LB2822.75 .B77 2024 (print) | LCC LB2822.75 (ebook) |
    DDC 371.26—dc23/eng/20230707
LC record available at https://lccn.loc.gov/2023026198
LC ebook record available at https://lccn.loc.gov/2023026199

33 32 31 30 29 28 27 26 25 24   1 2 3 4 5 6 7 8 9 10 11 12

I dedicate this book to my husband,
Frank Brookhart,
whose love and support I count on,
for this book and always.

Classroom Assessment Essentials

Acknowledgments

Education is a collaborative enterprise. We think and do, learn and grow together. In this regard, assessment is no different from other aspects of education. I acknowledge with gratitude the work and ideas of my colleagues in classroom assessment, many of whose works are listed in the "Further Reading" section of each chapter in this book. I acknowledge with gratitude the work of the teachers and students whose assessment experiences have shaped my understanding of real-world classroom assessment. And I acknowledge the future work of you, the reader, whose thoughts and actions will determine whether this book does, indeed, make a contribution to improving classroom assessment.

Acknowledgments

Introduction

Once, I observed in a 1st grade class that was copying some text from a model onto wide-ruled writing paper. One little girl, I'll call her Aisha, had a disturbed look on her face. One of her letters was improperly formed, and her teacher had told her it was wrong, which was true. In her mind, however, she had done the right thing and could not imagine what was wrong with her work. Something about my angle of approach or the angle of the model caught my attention, and without thinking I blurted out, "Oh, *I* see what you did!" I could tell how she could have quite reasonably created the letter improperly, not because of any vision problem but simply because that's the way the model appeared at that angle. I will never forget the look on her face, which changed so quickly from consternation to delight and cemented my commitment to encourage assessment practices that listen to students.

This seemingly trivial classroom assessment event helps illustrate the theme of this book. How do you find out what's happening with students who are learning so you can continue that learning? How do students get a sense of where they are and where they need to go next? The answer to both questions is assessment. The best classroom assessment helps teachers teach and students learn. In a nutshell, that's the theme of this book.

This theme has three corollaries. First, if assessment is to be helpful, it must provide accurate and relevant information at the time and in the form in which it is needed. Neither teachers nor students can make good decisions about learning if information is unsound, inaccurate, irrelevant, or unavailable. The judgment that Aisha's letter was wrong wasn't helpful information because it contraindicated what Aisha knew, that she had copied what she saw perfectly.

Second, the most helpful assessment gives both teachers *and* students usable information. At this point, educators know enough about how students learn to realize that if students passively wait for a teacher to tell them whether they know something or not, then they haven't really learned it. Aisha knew her copying was correct. That's why she was so disturbed when the teacher told her it was wrong.

Third, to do assessment well, teachers *and* students need the appropriate knowledge, skill, and will. I hope this book helps with all three: presenting assessment concepts to teachers, in a how-to form so they can practice, with enough success that they are motivated to make effective assessment a cornerstone of their classrooms. Not all students will be as self-aware as Aisha was in that moment. Effective assessment, however, can increase the number of students who monitor their own learning, their confidence, and ultimately their achievement.

This book is not a "book" in the traditional sense. That is, you don't need to read it from front to back. I envisioned it as a collection of quick references on a set of topics that, together, can form the basis for assessment literate teaching practice. Readers can select the topics they want to investigate and the order in which they want to read them. The selection of topics is my own, but it was informed by the work of other classroom assessment scholars and professional developers as well (Brookhart, 2011; DeLuca et al., 2016; JCSEE, 2015; McTighe & Ferrara, 2021; Pastore & Andrade, 2019; Xu & Brown, 2016).

The theme and its three corollaries are built into the design of each chapter. Each chapter has sections intended to share information about the topic, why it's important, how to do it, and how to involve students. Each chapter is brief enough to be read and implemented quickly (the "quick reference" aspect), and for that reason I had to be selective about what to include in each one. I used the "desert island" test to decide what information went in and what was left for another day; each chapter has a "For Further Reading" section. You've probably all played this game in your childhood: If I were going to be stranded on a desert island, what would I most want to take with me? For this book, my question was similar: Given the limited space available for each chapter, what content is so important that the topic is not properly treated without mentioning it? Much more information is available for each topic, and I encourage you to pursue further reading in each area if you can. Nevertheless, according to my desert island test, you could survive on what's in each chapter.

I invite you to jump in! Look at the table of contents and select a topic that is of interest to you right now. Read it, and then decide how it can and will affect your classroom assessment practice.

FOR FURTHER READING

Brookhart, S. M. (2011). Educational assessment knowledge and skills for teachers. *Educational Measurement: Issues and Practice, 30*(1), 3–12.

DeLuca, C., LaPointe-McEwan, D., & Luhanga, U. (2016). Teacher assessment literacy: A review of international standards and measures. *Educational Assessment, Evaluation and Accountability, 28*(3), 251–272.

Joint Committee on Standards for Educational Evaluation (JCSEE) (2015). *The classroom assessment standards for preK-12 teachers.* www.jcsee.org

McTighe, J., & Ferrara, S. (2021). *Assessing student learning by design.* Teachers College Press.

Pastore, S., & Andrade, H. L. (2019). Teacher assessment literacy: A three-dimensional model. *Teaching and Teacher Education, 84,* 128–138.

Xu, Y., & Brown, G. T. L. (2016). Teacher assessment literacy in practice: A reconceptualization. *Teaching and Teacher Education, 58,* 149–162.

1

Understanding the Formative Assessment Cycle

What Is the Formative Assessment Cycle?

Assessment is formative when its primary purpose is to inform teaching and learning—when it forms something. Assessment is summative when its primary purpose is to grade, certify, or report learning—when it sums up something. Some kinds of formative assessment can occur without students, for example, when a teacher uses results of an interim assessment for instructional planning. However, the kind of formative assessment that has been shown to be effective for learning involves students and happens in the classroom during learning (Black & Wiliam, 1998). It is sometimes called assessment *for* learning. This chapter describes this kind of student-involved classroom formative assessment, which plays out in what has been called the formative assessment cycle.

The formative assessment cycle, sometimes called the formative learning cycle, is typically expressed as three questions: Where am I going? Where am I now? Where to next? (or sometimes, How do I close the gap?) This cycle (see Figure 1.1) is a practical expression of what happens during students' regulation of learning.

Keeping the formative assessment cycle in mind as you are teaching will focus your formative assessment on students and their learning, which is what needs to happen if the much-touted benefits of formative assessment are to be realized in your classroom. Keeping the focus on students will help

FIGURE 1.1
The Formative Assessment Cycle

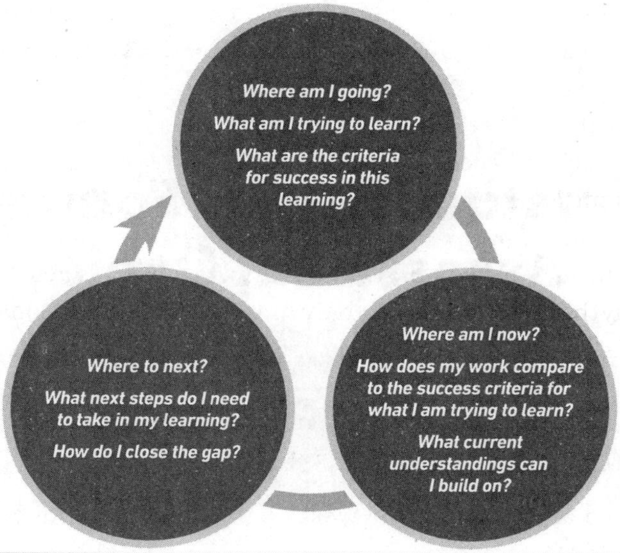

Source: From *The Formative Assessment Learning Cycle* (Quick Reference Guide) (p. 1), by S. M. Brookhart and J. McTighe, 2017, ASCD. Copyright 2017 by ASCD.

you keep the focus on learning. Fisher and Frey (2009, p. 21) have described this same cycle from the point of view of what the teacher does: "feed up, feed back, feed forward."

Why Is the Formative Assessment Cycle Important?

Self-regulation of learning, sometimes called "learning how to learn," is explained as both a mechanism by which students learn and a desired outcome itself. Self-regulation of learning happens when students set goals for their learning—or at least understand what the goals are—and muster cognitive, motivational, and behavioral strategies to meet them. As a simple example, consider a student trying to learn how to do multistep math problems that require two different operations (addition and multiplication, say). Cognitively, the student considers various problem-solving strategies and pays attention to how to figure out when to add and when to multiply. Motivationally, the student applies herself to the task, paying attention, willing herself to do assigned practice work, and so on. Behaviorally, the student might choose to persist in the work even if it's hard, to ask for help when needed, and so on. Typically, teachers want students to apply themselves to their learning in this way—that is, to use the formative assessment cycle—both so they learn the intended content and so they learn how to approach learning. None of that is possible if students do not understand what they are trying to learn and have no way to figure out where they are now and where to go next.

Contrast this self-regulated learner with a student who is merely complying with teacher directions, may or may not understand the goal of learning is to do multistep problems, and simply does what he is asked to do. The student may learn how to do multistep problems, through repetition if nothing else, but he may not be aware of exactly what it is he is able to do and may not learn anything about how to apply himself in future lessons.

How Do I Use the Formative Assessment Cycle in My Teaching and Assessment?

The formative assessment cycle works best in a classroom context where students feel safe to express their ideas and where mistakes are seen as opportunities to learn. Students do not learn all by themselves, but rather through social interaction with teachers and peers, the classroom context, and the content itself. In a learning-oriented classroom, students would feel safe, for example, to ask how to figure out what to add and what to multiply. In classes that emphasize sharing right answers, students might not feel safe to ask such a question, because it would mean they had to show they didn't know something.

Some strategies for valuing learning in a classroom include the following:

- Teach students that making mistakes is part of the learning process. Say this, explicitly. Comment on students' thinking when they share it, and help everyone see how the thinking led to the learning. Strategies like "my favorite no" (below) can help, too.
- Use learning-focused language all the time. Instead of emphasizing that something will be on a test, for example, or that something will please you ("What I need from you is..."), emphasize student thinking and learning ("How are you thinking about that?" "What are you trying to learn?").
- Give students helpful feedback, and opportunities to use it without penalty, to improve their work. Value the improvement (the learning) rather than the amount of time or practice it took to get there. Teach students to focus on how they will use the feedback to make their work

better, how to ask further questions if needed, and so on. If students perceive feedback as information to help them move forward, rather than criticism of what they have already done, they are participating in the formative assessment cycle.

• Teach students how to self-assess, and model that process yourself.

Figure 1.2 lists some strategies for classroom formative assessment. Most of them only work, or only work well, in a learning-oriented classroom, so it's a good idea to start by working on developing a learning-oriented classroom. However, using these strategies can be part of your efforts to shift the classroom climate in that direction.

Where Am I Going?

Because active learning requires that students have a goal, the most important formative assessment strategies clarify for students what they are trying to learn and what that looks like in their work. All classroom formative assessment strategies help clarify learning goals in some way, because as students get more and more information about their learning, they develop more nuanced ideas about what that learning is. Two formative assessment strategies specifically and primarily intended to focus on learning goals are sharing clear learning targets and success criteria (see Chapter 2) and using pre-assessment (see Chapter 3). Sharing clear learning targets and success criteria sets the formative learning cycle in motion for students.

FIGURE 1.2
Strategies for Classroom Formative Assessment

Where am I going? Strategies for starting on a learning journey
1. Sharing clear learning targets and success criteria
2. Pre-assessment (e.g., pretest, inventory, KWL chart, concept map, classroom discussion)
Where am I now? Strategies for checking for understanding during learning
3. Choosing (e.g., hand signals, colored cards or cups, student response systems)
4. Speaking (e.g., reflective toss, open-ended questions/discussion, protocols)
5. Writing (e.g., quick-writes, entrance/exit tickets, blank slides, question box)
6. Graphics (e.g., KWL, concept maps, Venn diagrams)
7. Solving (e.g., whiteboards, my favorite no, explain reasoning)
Where to next? Strategies for improving learning and next steps
8. Teacher feedback
9. Self-assessment
10. Peer assessment

It is the "breakfast of champions" that starts the day—the necessary food from which learning will grow.

Many teachers are used to thinking of pre-assessment as a way to gauge students' background knowledge for an upcoming unit or series of lessons. This is true as far as it goes, but the best pre-assessment also serves to give students an idea of what they will be trying to learn in that unit or series of lessons, and feedback on things to watch for as they do their studying and work.

Almost any of the strategies for checking for understanding during lessons can be used as pre-assessment (i.e., before lessons) as well as during lessons. In addition, teachers sometimes give a conventional pre-test to check for prior knowledge of facts and concepts or an inventory or survey to assess students' interest. Pre-tests should test what students know, not what they don't, to avoid starting a unit with a failure experience. Select a few key facts and concepts that will be most useful for planning. Don't grade pre-tests; students should not be held accountable for information they have not been taught. Review pre-tests by focusing on what students know and how they are thinking about key concepts and use that information to support differentiated instruction.

Where Am I Now?

The formative assessment cycle is fueled by information. When students do learning and assessment activities that are closely matched with the daily learning target and part of a trajectory toward a longer-term learning goal, they not only learn, but they produce evidence of learning. Think of a simple example. Students who are trying to learn to write effective persuasive essays practice writing those essays, using targets (taking a clear position, providing clear support for the position, etc.) and criteria (e.g., from a rubric for persuasive writing). As they do this, they learn—and they also produce essays that can be assessed.

Teachers can develop a repertoire of information-gathering techniques that are useful during learning to give students and teachers a quick check for understanding. Most of them are useful for pre-assessment, as well. Use these formative assessment strategies regularly, typically at least once during each lesson.

Each of the strategies for checking for understanding in Figure 1.2 depends on a question or prompt to which students respond. In every case, the quality of the formative assessment information depends directly on the quality of that question or prompt. Figure 1.2 organizes these strategies according to the kind of response students make.

Some questions call for students to select a response. These can be multiple-choice or true-false questions about content or questions about student confidence in their understanding. Students can indicate their choices with hand signals (e.g., thumbs up, down, or sideways; fist-to-five), with colored cards or cups (red-yellow-green), with electronic student response systems (sometimes called "clickers"), or with other app-based or web-based quiz software.

Oral questions in class call for students to speak their answers. Various question-and-answer or discussion facilitation methods can be used. The best questions are directly matched with important learning goals; require student thinking, not just recall; and provide a way in for a wide range of student responses. Brief written responses can be especially useful when you need to review answers later—as opposed to on-the-fly during a lesson—or when it would be helpful to students to take the time to think and write a response, whether on paper, by using web-based audience response software, or by using a Google form. Examples include entrance or exit tickets, quick-writes, blank slides, and question box. Some checks for understanding use graphic organizers (e.g., KWL charts, Venn diagrams) or student-constructed graphics (e.g., concept maps) where students diagram their answers to a question.

Several methods can be used for surveying class problem solving. These are often used in mathematics classes, but they can be adapted to any class in which the learning goal involves being able to solve problems. Examples include individual whiteboards and exercises like "my favorite no" or any other where the task includes having students explain their reasoning. For individual whiteboards, post a problem for students to solve, give them an appropriate amount of time, and then ask them to hold up their whiteboards. A quick scan of the room will give you information about how students are doing and what kinds of problems, if any, they are having.

"My favorite no" (demonstrated in this video https://vimeo.com/383597686 by math teacher Leah Alcala) is a routine to help students explain their thinking on a problem. The teacher poses a problem, typically as an entrance or exit ticket, and has students solve it on an index card anonymously. Collect the cards and quickly sort them into two piles: Yes (correct answers) and No (incorrect answers). Choose one of the No cards to be your favorite no; choose an example that will allow students to talk about a common misconception or something that might be a trouble spot for the group. Post the problem using a document reader or, to further anonymize, copy it onto a whiteboard. Facilitate a discussion about the problem: What was done correctly? What is incorrect (the "No")? Why is this my favorite No (what does it help us learn about this concept or kind of problem)? It helps to give students some pair-discussion time first, so that they have something to say when the discussion begins.

The type of question to which you want students to respond should dictate your choice of strategy. For example, if you want students to indicate whether they think a cork will float or sink in water, thumbs up/down would work well. If you want students to explain why the cork will float or sink, a quick-write would work better.

Where to Next?

Students can take next steps in learning in several ways. They can revise work or change the focus of their studying. They can shift the way they understand a concept, perhaps with an "aha!" moment or perhaps with carefully coached rethinking. They can go deeper, adding concepts and connections to their schema—their way of understanding—of a concept or topic. They can get information to support these next steps from self-assessment, teacher feedback, or peer assessment.

Student self-assessment is one of the hallmarks of the formative assessment cycle. Armed with a shared understanding of learning goals and criteria, students who self-assess both improve in the content area and develop their capabilities as self-regulated learners. Every lesson should include an opportunity for students to take stock of their learning, using criteria. This will keep students feeding their learning forward.

The most effective teacher feedback describes the strengths of students' current work in terms of shared criteria, makes a suggestion for next steps, and then provides students an opportunity to use the feedback. In other words, the best teacher feedback includes some additional lesson plans.

The greatest benefit of peer assessment is that the peer assessor gets a clearer understanding of the learning target. When students look at the work of their classmates, they see another example of what it means to work toward the learning goal, and in the process can better understand their own progress.

How Do I Involve Students in the Formative Assessment Cycle?

All formative assessment strategies involve students in some way, as you can see. For student involvement to be effective, students must have three things. The most important thing about involving students is starting out with clear learning targets and success criteria. Students can only engage in the formative learning cycle if they have a clear idea of the goal for learning. They can only move toward something if they have some idea of what the "something" is, at the level of someone who has not yet learned it.

Second, they must have a sense that their thinking, and their decisions about their learning, matter. Listening to students is critical. Really listen, figure out what they really mean and how they are thinking, and then respond to that. Use the language of the learning target and success criteria to help students develop clarity about what they mean.

Third, the process of instruction and assessment during lessons must be structured to allow for students to see their work in terms of where they are going, where they are now, and where they should go next. That means you need assignments that clearly match lesson learning targets, a clear progression lesson-by-lesson that is leading toward a larger learning goal, and pause points and feedback that allow students to take next steps with the appropriate level of scaffolding.

What Are Some Common Misconceptions About the Formative Assessment Cycle?

In this author's experience, two common misconceptions cause the most harm to the whole idea of formative assessment. The first is that formative assessment is a certain kind of test. The point of this chapter has been understanding the formative assessment cycle, which is a process. To be sure, it is based on information from assessments, some of which can be tests, and these assessments must be of high quality to yield useful information. What makes assessment information formative is that it is used formatively, that is, when it contributes to students' participation in a formative learning cycle toward a desired learning goal.

A second common misconception is not exactly a misconception, it's more of a misplaced attribution. Sometimes the benefits of classroom formative assessment, which engage students' self-regulation of learning—what this chapter has called the formative learning cycle—are mistakenly attributed to the interim assessments required by some schools and districts or to the common formative assessments sometimes administered across classrooms within a school or district. So, for example, you may have heard educators say that their school gave "formative assessments" and that they expected that to increase achievement. That "s" on the end of the word assessments is a clue that the speaker is thinking about formative assessment as a type of test. Although information from interim assessments can be used formatively, if, for example, teachers use it to improve their instructional plans for the next time they teach a topic, there is no evidence that this formative use actually improves achievement (Hill, 2020), as there is for classroom formative assessment. The main point of this chapter is that student achievement improves when students know where they are going, where they are now, and where to go next in their learning. Student achievement improves with classroom formative assessment based on the formative learning cycle.

FOR FURTHER READING

Black, P., & Wiliam, D. (1998). Inside the black box: Raising standards through classroom assessment. *Phi Delta Kappan, 80,* 139–148.

Brookhart, S. (2020, May). *Five formative assessment strategies to improve distance learning outcomes for students with disabilities* (NCEO Brief #20). National Center on Educational Outcomes. https://nceo.umn.edu/docs/OnlinePubs/NCEOBrief20.pdf

Brookhart, S. M., & McTighe, J. (2017). *The formative assessment learning cycle* (quick reference guide). ASCD.

Chappuis, J. (2015). *Seven strategies of assessment for learning* (2nd ed.). Pearson.

Fisher, D., & Frey, N. (2009). Feed up, back, forward. *Educational Leadership, 67*(3), 20–25. https://www.ascd.org/el/articles/feed-up-back-forward

Fisher, D., & Frey, N. (2014). *Checking for understanding: Formative assessment techniques for your classroom* (2nd ed.). ASCD.

Frey, N., Hattie, J., & Fisher, D. (2018). *Developing assessment-capable visible learners, grades K–12.* Corwin.

Hill, H. C. (2020, February 7). Does studying student data really raise test scores? *Education Week.* https://www.edweek.org/technology/opinion-does-studying-student-data-really-raise-test-scores/2020/02

Moss, C. M., & Brookhart, S. M. (2019). *Advancing formative assessment in every classroom* (2nd ed.). ASCD.

Wiliam, D., & Leahy, S. (2015). *Embedding formative assessment.* Learning Sciences International.

2

Teaching with Learning Targets and Success Criteria

What Are Learning Targets and Success Criteria?

A lesson has a learning target when students know what they are aiming to learn and are, in fact, aiming to learn it. Three elements help that to happen:

1. A *learning target statement* helps articulate for students what it is they are going to learn. A learning target statement describes what students will learn in today's lesson, in language that students can understand, from the point of view of a student who is learning it for the first time.
2. A *performance of understanding* is something students will do, make, say, or write during the lesson that will help them learn and also produce evidence of learning that students and teachers can see.
3. *Success criteria*, sometimes called "look-fors," are qualities to look for in students' work that help monitor progress toward the target and gauge learning.

All three of these elements, together, make it likely that students will get a concept of what they are trying to learn and see their way clear to aim for it.

Why Are Learning Targets and Success Criteria Important?

The first step in activating the formative learning cycle is to communicate clearly to students what they will be learning in the long term (e.g., standards or unit goals), what they should expect to learn in the present lesson (today's learning target), how it will help them approach the larger goal, and how they will know they are learning. In other words, learning targets and success criteria are important because they help students take ownership of and regulate their learning. Without a learning goal, students can comply with directions but cannot truly aim to learn something. Learning targets and success criteria are also important because they can be an agent for equity in the classroom. In lessons that are designed using a learning target theory of action, all students, not just some, have access to the goals for learning and the criteria for good work.

Lesson learning targets and success criteria are the means by which students apprehend what it is they are trying to learn in a lesson and how they will know they are learning. They are student-facing, written in student-friendly language and accessible by students who have not yet achieved the intended learning outcomes for a lesson. They are the foundation for all other formative assessment practices. They are derived from larger curriculum learning goals or standards and, lesson by lesson, define a learning trajectory toward those goals.

How Do I Use Learning Targets and Success Criteria in My Teaching and Assessment?

Sharing lesson learning targets typically starts with a statement (e.g., "Today we are learning to count by 2s," or "I can explain the difference between supply and demand and the relationship between them") to focus students' efforts during the lesson. But the statement alone is not enough. It needs to be coupled with, and explicitly connected to, something students will do during the lesson (a performance where students can develop and demonstrate understanding). Sometimes these are called "learning activities," although not every learning activity is a performance of understanding. The activity must not only help students learn, it must also produce evidence of that learning. The learning target and performance of understanding should be coupled with one or more criteria students and teachers both can use as evidence of learning that will show in students' work. This section will discuss the three elements separately, but it's important to remember that all three are necessary.

Learning Target Statement

A learning target statement uses language to help students think about what they are trying to learn. The language should be student-friendly, which means more than using simple vocabulary. Similarly, speaking from a student's point of view means more than using first person. Couch the statement in terms that a student would actually use. Edit the statement to be clear and concise—with "clear" meaning clear to the student. Finally, make sure the statement describes what students will *learn* from a lesson, not what they will *do* during the lesson. If you find yourself writing a "do" statement, ask yourself, "What will the student learn by doing this?" Figure 2.1 gives some examples of clear, student-friendly learning target statements.

Review the learning target statement with students, either at the start of the lesson or at an appropriate point (e.g., in a discovery lesson after students think they have "discovered" something). It may be posted on the board, but it should also be actively reviewed. For example, it can be unpacked in classroom discussion or a turn-and-talk moment. In classrooms where students keep a learning journal, the learning target statement can be copied at the start of the day's entry. Highlight content-relevant vocabulary and give students an opportunity to ask questions.

Performance of Understanding

In every lesson, students should do, make, say, or write something to help them learn and to give evidence of learning. This performance also helps clarify the goal itself by exemplifying or illustrating it. A student might think, "Learning this concept or skill means being able to do work like this." To extend the target metaphor, if the learning target is what students are aiming for, the performance of understanding puts the bow and arrow in their hands.

What students do, make, say, or write should be a clear match with the learning target. To give an obvious example, if students are supposed to be learning how imagery can be used to support the theme of a poem, then the performance of understanding could be analyzing the imagery in a poem and relating it to its theme. If, instead, the lesson asked students to mark out the meter of the poem, that would not be a match and would not help much to move students closer to their learning goal. Use the language of the learning target as you describe the assignment and as you talk with students while they are doing it.

One of the most common "near misses" in the quest to match the performance of understanding with the learning goal happens when what students do during the lesson seems on topic but is not an exact match. Suppose students were learning about fables. In their series of lessons about fables, they first studied characterization—in a fable, the characters are usually animals with human characteristics—for several lessons. Then they had several lessons about the moral of a fable, as fables usually are stories

FIGURE 2.1

Examples of Learning Targets for Daily Lessons

	Learning Target Statement	**Performance of Understanding**	**Success Criteria**
Primary Example	I can write a capital E.	Students write several Es on lined paper, copying a model.	A model capital E shows what to look for. Students are prompted to ask themselves, "Does my letter look like the model?"
Elementary Math Example	Today we are learning how to look at a subtraction problem to figure out whether we need to use regrouping.	Students complete a problem set containing two-digit subtraction problems, some of which need regrouping and some of which do not.	Students use a subtraction rap: "More on top, no need to stop. More on the floor, go next door."
Middle School ELA Example	Today we are learning how and why an author uses flashbacks in stories.	Students read and analyze a piece of narrative text that uses flashbacks.	• Can I find the shift in time in the story? Can I explain the transition that cued this shift in time? • Can I explain why the author chose a particular event to flash back to? • Can I explain how a flashback helps develop some aspect of the story (e.g., character, mood, or theme)? • Can I put the events of the story in chronological order?
Secondary Geography Example	Today we are learning that all maps are distorted in different ways based on the perspective of the cartographer.	Students examine different world maps and identify the distortions in each. They explain how the maps show the distortions.	• Can I identify and describe four types of distortions (size, shape, direction, distance)? • Can I find an example of one of those distortions on the map? • Can I name the part of the map that shows the distortion and explain why?
Physical Education Example	I can throw and catch a baseball with appropriate overhand technique and accuracy.	Students play catch with partners.	• For throwing technique, modeling or a checklist is used. My throwing looks like the model (or matches the checklist). • I drop no more than 3 out of 10 catches.

Note: Each of these examples would take its place in a series of lessons toward a larger learning goal. The next learning target in the series would change at least one element (statement, performance, or criteria), and students should understand how the previous lesson prepared them for this new step.

that convey a moral. For one of the characterization lessons, students read Aesop's fable, "The Ant and the Grasshopper." A performance of understanding might be: "Three students picked different words to describe the grasshopper. The words they picked were lazy, short-sighted, and talkative. Which student do you think picked the best word to describe the grasshopper? Explain your thinking and use details from the fable to support your choice." Another performance, about the same fable but not directly about characterization, would not embody the learning target if, for example, you asked students to write their own fable about the virtues of hard work and planning for the future, or if you asked groups of students to act out the fable in a skit for the class.

When the performance of understanding does match the learning target, students are supported in their formative learning cycle. Note, too, that not everything students do, make, say, or write during a lesson is a performance of understanding. Sometimes, for example, lessons begin with a review of relevant vocabulary, or a discussion of yesterday's learning target and how it led to today's. Sometimes students perform routines that are important for the class but not tied to the day's learning target, for example, washing their hands after using paints. The key is that at least one of the activities in a lesson is a performance of understanding, and students know what it is. Figure 2.1 gives some examples.

Success Criteria

Students need to know what to look for in their work to monitor their progress and make midcourse corrections, or even just to feel like they are in charge of their own learning process. Success criteria, sometimes called "look-fors," serve this purpose. Success criteria may be formatted and shared with students in many different ways, including a list of "I can" statements, rubrics, checklists, guiding questions, exemplars, models, and demonstrations. Which to choose depends on the content, student developmental level, and where students are in a trajectory toward a larger learning goal. In any case, success criteria should be qualities students—and you—can look for in their work to decide how well they are progressing toward the learning target.

As for learning target statements, use student-friendly language in the success criteria. Use language that describes the work (e.g., "the same number of each type of atom is on both sides of the equation," for a lesson on balancing chemical equations), rather than evaluative language ("the equations are correct"). For cognitive learning outcomes, do not count (e.g., "has fewer than three grammar errors") but rather describe ("grammar errors do not interfere with meaning"). Counting gives some teachers and students a false sense of equity, because some feel it's easy to apply the criteria to everyone in the same manner. Actually, this is not true. Three obscure grammar errors in a long, complex essay are not the same as three simple errors in a three-sentence paragraph, for example. For this reason, criteria that involve counting often mismeasure student achievement. As an aside—for criteria about physical skills or other learning outcomes in the psychomotor domain, counting works (e.g., "broad-jumped 5 feet," "keyboarded 60 words per minute," or as in the catching example in Figure 2.1, "I drop no more than 3 out of 10 catches"). For criteria about behaviors, counting works (e.g., "came prepared for class 90 percent of the time"). But for the kind of learning in most content areas, counting not only does not work, it also often misrepresents learning.

Select aspects of the work that will demonstrate learning, not following directions. If you need a directions checklist you can use that as well, but elements of the directions (e.g., "has a title," "name on paper," "neat not sloppy") are not success criteria that indicate progress toward the learning target. Figure 2.1 gives some examples of success criteria that students can use to clarify their understanding of the learning target and monitor their progress toward it. How effectively students can use the learning target statement and criteria depends in part on how clearly and appropriately they are expressed.

Building or Growing Competence

It is fairly easy to see a trajectory toward a standard in lesson learning target statements. For example, an 8th grade mathematics teacher planned a trajectory toward the goal of students understanding the Pythagorean theorem in geometry. Here are the six learning target statements he used, culminating in lesson 6 with the complete goal for the series of lessons.

- Lesson 1: I can discover how the sides of a triangle are related mathematically. (Discovery lesson to arrive at $a^2 + b^2 = c^2$)
- Lesson 2: I can figure out whether a triangle is a right triangle. (Seeing whether it satisfies $a^2 + b^2 = c^2$)
- Lesson 3: I can find the length of the hypotenuse of a right triangle if I know the length of two legs.
- Lesson 4: I can find the length of a leg of a right triangle if I know the length of the hypotenuse and the other leg.
- Lesson 5: I can figure out whether a missing side of a right triangle is a hypotenuse or leg and find its length.
- Lesson 6: I can solve real-world problems with the Pythagorean Theorem.

This example shows how bite-size (lesson-size) bits of learning described in learning target statements build on each other and add up to a larger learning goal. It can be hard at first for teachers to be able to articulate the lesson-size learning goals, if they are only used to focusing on larger learning goals. In general, though, the issue of a trajectory of learning targets is not a difficult concept to grasp.

It is sometimes more difficult to create a learning trajectory in the success criteria. Doing so requires thinking about the relationship between lesson success criteria and the criteria for assessing whether students have met the larger goal at the end of the unit or series of lessons. For example, a unit's culminating activity might be a complex performance assessment matched to the learning goal, with a set of rubrics. There are at least four ways that individual lesson learning criteria can "roll up" to criteria for a larger learning goal. Think of the metaphors of building or growing. Some of these ways build (e.g., adding one criterion at a time), and some grow (e.g., using simple criteria for novices that fold into a more complex criterion for mastery) student competence.

1. **Develop one criterion at a time in lessons, then put them together in a culminating complex performance**. For example, teachers who teach writing using the Six-Trait Rubrics are advised to concentrate on one criterion at a time (e.g., Ideas). Similarly, math problem solving can be taught by focusing on one criterion (e.g., Explaining Reasoning). I once worked with a visual arts teacher who taught a series of lessons on developing a good landscape with a sequence of lessons that taught composition first (e.g., fill in the whole space), then how to draw parts of a landscape (e.g., trees, rocks), and then craftsmanship, culminating in an assignment to create a landscape using all the criteria.

2. **Introduce new criteria into lessons gradually, keeping the previous ones**. Sometimes teachers work on one criterion at a time but, once introduced, they also pay attention to previously introduced criteria. This approach can be used, for example, with writing rubrics or with vocal performance in music (working on pitch, rhythm, tone, diction, and interpretation/dynamics).

3. **Think in developmental terms (novice, developing, mastering).** This approach is often taken for series of lessons that work on developing fluency (e.g., oral reading, playing a musical instrument), memory or mastery (e.g., math facts), or increasing proficiency (e.g., practicing the same skill with more complex problems each lesson or

more complex text). Success criteria for introductory lessons when students are novices can require only novice-level performance, and increase in development, culminating in criteria for final assessment of the standard.

4. **Work on parts of a complex criterion with simpler success criteria that roll up into a more complex description.** Sometimes lesson criteria are finer-grained than the criteria for mastery of a whole standard. For example, in elementary language arts, sentencing skills (capital, period, complete thought) might be taught individually and eventually just called sentencing skills, leading ultimately to "mechanics" or "grammar" in later years. Or lessons with scaffolded math criteria (e.g., circle the numbers, identify key words) eventually roll up to "represent the problem."

None of these strategies is better than the others; the important thing is that the strategy you choose is appropriate for your purposes. Use a strategy for creating trajectories of learning targets and success criteria that make sense with the content you are trying to teach and the students in your class.

How Do I Involve Students in My Teaching and Assessment?

The key to involving students in using learning targets and success criteria—and therefore moving into the formative learning cycle—is to communicate the learning target many times during the lesson, use the language of the learning target and success criteria in your classroom talk, and give students opportunities to do the same. Reading a learning target aloud off the board and never referring to it again will not keep it top of mind for students. Remember, it's a "target" because students are aiming for it, not because you wrote it on the board.

Once students know, or think they know, what it is they are meant to be learning in a lesson, the most powerful student involvement comes when students use the success criteria themselves. Using pause points during the lesson, giving students opportunities to share their thinking, having them do self-reflection during and after working, and providing opportunities for self-assessment of their work are all strategies that require students to use the criteria. That's why it's so important that the criteria are in student-friendly language and in a useful format. If students do not use the success criteria, they will not have the information they need to regulate their learning, for example, looking over a problem a second time, rereading a paragraph that didn't seem clear, asking for help when needed, and so on. Just as importantly, if students do not use the success criteria, they will not have the information they need to develop confidence in themselves as learners, realizing what it is they have just learned and how well they have learned it.

What Are Some Common Misconceptions About Learning Targets and Success Criteria?

Probably the most common misconception about learning targets is that the target is a statement. Some people even go so far as to say the target must be an "I can" statement. Similarly, learning targets are not just teacher instructional objectives edited to be "I can" statements. A learning target is something students are aiming for and that teachers are helping students aim for. If a supervisor or coach wanted to know whether a lesson had a learning target, checking to see whether an "I can" statement is written on the board would not answer the question. Rather, they could ask several different students "What are you trying to learn in this lesson?" and see what story their answers told.

The most common misconception about success criteria is that they can be described as something students achieve—for example, get at least 80 percent of a set of problems correct, or write an effective descriptive paragraph. When you run into criteria like this, ask yourself, "What would a student have to understand in order to get most of the problems correct?" or "What makes a descriptive paragraph effective?" This is the kind of information students need in order to make progress toward their learning goal.

FOR FURTHER READING

Brookhart, S. M., & Moss, C. M. (2014). Learning targets on parade. *Educational Leadership, 72*(2), 28–33. https://www.ascd.org/el/articles/learning-targets-on-parade

Dueck, M. (2021). *Giving students a say: Smarter assessment practices to empower and engage.* ASCD.

Fisher, D., & Frey, N. (2011). *The purposeful classroom: How to structure lessons with learning goals in mind.* ASCD.

Moss, C. M., & Brookhart, C. M. (2012). *Learning targets: Helping students aim for understanding in today's lesson.* ASCD.

3

Starting with Pre-Assessment

What Is Pre-Assessment?

Pre-assessment is a type of formative assessment used before instruction to support teacher instructional planning and inform students about what they will be learning. Pre-assessment may be used to identify the knowledge, skills, experiences, or dispositions students bring to a new unit of instruction or sequence of lessons. It is particularly useful for supporting differentiation of instruction. Successful pre-assessment gives information to both the teacher and the students.

Why Is Pre-Assessment Important?

Pre-assessment addresses the intended learning goals for an upcoming unit or series of lessons. For a given learning goal, information may be sought about one or more of the following: students' prior experiences (in school or out) with the concepts or topic; interest; personal connections; general knowledge; specific prerequisite knowledge or skills; knowledge of vocabulary or key terms; and knowledge of concepts, skills, or procedures to be taught. This information helps teachers plan instruction for all students and make sure that instruction and assessment are relevant to students' lived experiences. It is especially useful for deciding on instructional timing and pacing—spending less time on concepts students are familiar with and more time on unfamiliar content—and for differentiating instruction. The information can be used for grouping. For example, in my own teaching I have successfully grouped students heterogeneously by interest, so that each group contained students who were more and less interested, and found that with effective group assignments, interest can be contagious.

From the students' perspective, pre-assessment can serve as "pre-emptive formative assessment" (Carless, 2007, p. 171). This means that pre-assessment can signal to students what it is they are going to be learning and what kinds of questions they will be able to answer, so they can begin to focus their thinking and set expectations.

A caution is in order here. Conventional "pre-tests" that contain similar questions to those that would be asked at the end of instruction, to find out "how much" of the material students already know, are not typically a good use of pre-assessment time. It is likely that students know very little about what they have not yet been taught, and a conventional pre-test can start a unit or series of lessons with a failure experience for many students. This type of pre-test is really a test of what students don't know. Effective pre-assessment attempts to find out what students do know and in the process show them how some things they already know will feed them into the upcoming lessons. For typical classroom units of instruction, other kinds of pre-assessment, like those in the following section, are better choices than conventional pre-tests.

How Do I Use Pre-Assessment in My Teaching and Assessment?

Examine the intended learning goals for an upcoming unit or series of lessons. Given those learning goals, what few things would be very helpful to know as you plan the unit? Use your knowledge of the content to be taught and the students in your class to decide what particular knowledge and skills would best help you make the specific decisions that would be most helpful. Are you planning some group work and are thinking it would be helpful to gauge student interest in order to form the groups? Are there some key prerequisite concepts for which, in your experience, students often have a range of understandings, and knowing that would help you differentiate instruction? Do the standards you are teaching build on previous standards (as, e.g., some ELA and mathematics standards do), so that it would be helpful for you to know how students are already performing?

Based on this preplanning exercise, decide what you most want to know. Depending on that purpose, select a pre-assessment strategy. The strategies in Figure 3.1 come from two sources (Brookhart & Lazarus, 2020; Brookhart

FIGURE 3.1
Strategies for Pre-Assessment

Primary Purpose	Strategy	Example
Assessing prior knowledge	Oral questioning or introductory discussion	Show young children a collection of leaves. Facilitate a discussion about what they already know about leaves or what they notice now.
	Brainstorming	Ask "What do living things need?" and record answers on chart paper or bulletin board software.
	KWL chart	Make a KWL chart to record what students know and want to know about the water cycle.
	Individual or small-group task	Give each group two graphs: a bar and line graph that both display number of ice cream cones sold per day. Ask them to interpret the graphs and explain which is more useful for displaying this information and why.
	Misconception check	Show students several diagrams of the movement of planets and ask them to identify which are examples of rotation and revolution.
	Single multiple-choice question with distractors based on common misconceptions	Write a question that asks whether and why a cork will float in water. Include three choices: the correct answer and two choices that reflect common misconceptions about floating and sinking.
	Concept map	Build a concept map around the term "migratory birds."
	Venn diagram	Label two overlapping circles "plant cells" and "animal cells." Ask students to fill in what they know.
Assessing prerequisite skills	Skills check	Present questions that require students to use an online card catalog and a rubric for them to self-assess their level of skill.
Assessing prior knowledge or interest, attitudes, and personal connections	Journal or quick-write prompt	Before a unit on recycling, ask students to write briefly about their experiences recycling at home.
Assessing interest and attitudes	Interest inventory	Administer a questionnaire asking students to rate their interest, on a scale of 1 to 5, on learning about key aspects of the next unit of instruction.
(Assessing prior knowledge)	Pre-test or quiz	Administer a test or quiz that asks similar questions to those that will be on the final unit test.

& McTighe, 2017). Use one of these or another assessment strategy that will answer your instructional planning questions and help students get a sense of what they will be learning, while developing student interest. Finally, make sure to close the loop: revisit your instructional plans after you learn more about students' thinking. As appropriate, especially as you are sharing learning targets during the unit or series of lessons, remind students about what they learned from the pre-assessment.

Oral Questioning or Introductory Discussion

Identify a key concept about which you want to know how students are thinking. Create one or more open questions—questions with more than one good answer. Or, if you need to ask a question that does have a right answer, ask students to explain their reasoning. Facilitate a brief discussion by having students respond to each other, and make sure to call on a range of students. Chapter 6 includes some ways to do that. The information you get will be at the class level, that is, you will have a sense of how the class as a whole is thinking, not specific information about any one individual.

Brainstorming

If you have one key question, consider a brainstorming session instead of a discussion. Prepare a focused, open question. Give students some "think time" (use no-hands-up time or a similar strategy), and then have students note their responses on newsprint, a whiteboard, or a bulletin board app. For younger students or any students who cannot write, you can scribe their responses. You can use the list as is, or you can have students sort and organize it in different ways, depending on what you and they need to know. Like an oral discussion, brainstorming yields information at the class level.

KWL Chart

The KWL chart (Ogle, 1986) is an "oldie but goodie." It was originally developed to help students read expository text, but it has been used since in many ways, notably—because it starts with what students Know and Want to Know—in pre-assessment in many content areas. Have students individually or in groups focus on a topic (e.g., the water cycle) using three columns (on paper or in a digital format such as a Google form): What I know (K), What I want to know (W), and what I learned (L). For pre-assessment, use the first two columns, then save the charts for reflection using the third column at the end of the unit or series of lessons. If students have trouble responding, revise the topic to be broader (e.g., water) until everyone has something to say. KWL charts can yield information at the group or individual level, depending on how you use them.

Individual or Small-Group Task

Assigning a task to individuals or small groups of students is a versatile way to collect all sorts of information. Some of the other strategies in this list (brainstorming, KWL charts, misconception check, skills check, concept map, Venn diagram) can be used as group or individual tasks. But this method can also be used to have students solve problems, create products, or do samples of the kind of work that will be upcoming. For example, if you are about to teach students a series of lessons on bar graphs and line graphs, you might give each small group two graphs charting the same information both ways (e.g., number of ice cream cones sold per day), and ask them to list all the things they can think of that the graphs tell them, concluding at the end which graph seems best suited to showing the information about ice cream sales. In addition to providing useful information at the group level, this activity engages students in academic talk about graphs and gives them an idea about what purposes graphs can serve.

Misconception Check

Identify a common misconception or error that often occurs when you teach an upcoming concept or skill. Show students an example of fictional student work containing this error or exhibiting this misconception and ask them to explain how the work is flawed. Misconceptions can also be presented as a true-false style list of statements; for each, students agree or disagree and explain their reasoning.

Single Multiple-Choice Question with Distractors Based on Common Misconceptions

You can create a version of a misconception check by writing one multiple-choice question with a correct answer choice and other choices based on common errors or misconceptions. The question can help you gauge not only who can get the question correct, but also what basic misconception may be held by the students who get it wrong. Information at the group level is available by looking at the distribution of student responses, which is easy to do in a student response system or quiz app.

Concept Map

A concept map, sometimes called a concept web, diagrams the relationships between a central concept and other concepts. A concept map is most useful when the information you need is students' prior understandings of one key concept from an upcoming unit or series of lessons. Students place the central concept in the center of a paper, whiteboard, newsprint, or concept mapping software and then connect the central concept to others. Students mark each connection with a line or arrow and, if possible, name the relationship (e.g., "contains," "causes"). Concept maps yield more information when done as a small-group task than when done individually, because the discussions students have while making the maps are informative. Making a concept map should help students realize what they already know about the concept they will be studying, as well. If desired, students can save their pre-assessment concept maps and compare them with the more mature maps they will make after their unit of study, to help them reflect on what they have learned.

Venn Diagram

A Venn diagram is a visual organizer that is useful for comparing and contrasting two or more concepts or topics. Like concept maps, Venn diagrams can serve as advance organizers for students, showing them that they already know about something they are about to study. In the simplest case, two overlapping circles are labeled with two related concepts or topics (e.g., "plant cells," "animal cells"). Characteristics of one concept but not the other are noted in the non-overlapping portions of the respective circles, and characteristics common to both are noted in the overlapping part. More complex Venn diagrams can be made with three or four overlapping circles. Because pre-assessment usually seeks to identify prior knowledge, often a simple Venn diagram with two key related concepts is sufficient. As with brainstorm lists and concept maps, a Venn diagram can be made by an individual or small group, depending on your purpose.

Skills Check

Have students check their own proficiency with a particular skill or process they have been taught. Prepare a checklist or rubric they can use for this purpose. Examples of skills students might check in this manner include using an electronic card catalog, making a wet mount slide for a microscope, and dribbling a basketball.

Journal or Quick-Write Prompt

If the information you need can be elicited via a writing prompt, consider using a quick-write. Craft a question that can be answered in a few sentences, and then give students a few minutes to write in their learning journal, on paper, into a bulletin board app, or in any manner that effectively puts the information where you and the students have good access to it. This method does yield information at the individual level, but because it is so brief the information may not be comprehensive. If the question is interesting, it can get students thinking and activating prior knowledge.

Interest Inventory

Sometimes a simple interest inventory or attitude survey helps teachers gauge interest or form small groups. A simple rating scale (e.g., "How interested are you in whales: Not at all, Some, A great deal?") can help you form groups that include a mixture of levels of interest, to maximize the experience students may have as they begin to work together. As a college professor teaching quantitative methods courses to educators, I used to form work groups heterogeneously by level of self-reported math anxiety. It worked like a charm. Every group had at least one person in it who wasn't afraid of the material and at least one person who would ask clarifying questions, making lots of room for explanatory talk.

Pre-Test or Quiz

It is certainly possible to give students a conventional pre-test or quiz to check for prior knowledge of key facts and concepts they will need in their upcoming unit. That information can help you decide what to emphasize, what can be skipped or simply reviewed, and so on. However, if it is possible to get the same information from an individual or small-group task, you may find that's a better introduction to the unit for students, producing more information and less anxiety than a pre-test. If you do decide a pre-test is in order, make it short, selecting only that prior knowledge that is essential for your planning purposes.

How Do I Involve Students in Pre-Assessment?

If pre-assessment seems to students like you are just using it for your instructional planning—that is, that you are "checking up" on them to see where they stand—you have missed a golden opportunity to involve students and to show them what *their* upcoming learning journey might look like. Use pre-assessment as part of your strategy to communicate the larger learning goal for the unit or series of lessons. Share that goal, explicitly, and then explain how the discussion or quick-write or group task or whatever pre-assessment you use will serve as a first step to show what they'll be thinking about in the coming lessons. Be true to the formative purpose of pre-assessment and do not grade it. If it makes sense, debrief the pre-assessment with a quick discussion about what students think they might be about to learn or what kinds of work they might end up being able to do.

Some kinds of pre-assessment can become part of student self-reflection at the end of the unit or series of lessons. For example, if students do a concept map before a unit on forces and motion, they can look back on what they constructed and reflect on what they've learned since.

What Are Some Common Misconceptions About Pre-Assessment?

One misconception has already been addressed: effective pre-assessment is not, typically, a pre-test over all the material to be taught. The kind of pre-assessment recommended in this chapter aims to find out what students know, not what they don't know, by posing questions or tasks that gauge students' background, interests, and prerequisite knowledge and skills.

A second misconception is a corollary of the first. Pre-assessment does not need to cover everything that is going to be taught in an upcoming unit or series of lessons in order to be useful for teachers for planning and for students to set expectations for what they are about to study. Focusing on a few key prerequisite skills, concepts, vocabulary, or experiences will give you a place to start in your instructional planning. Ongoing formative assessment during the unit will fill in the details as needed, in a timelier fashion than gathering that information all at the beginning. Focusing on those few key things will also help students get a clear general picture of what they are about to learn, uncluttered with details they do not yet have ways to organize.

FOR FURTHER READING

Brookhart, S., & Lazarus, S. S. (2020, December). *Pre-assessment to plan instruction for students with disabilities during distance learning* (NCEO Brief #21). National Center on Educational Outcomes.

Brookhart, S. M., & McTighe, J. (2017). *The formative assessment learning cycle* (quick reference guide). ASCD.

Carless, D. (2007). Conceptualizing pre-emptive formative assessment. *Assessment in Education: Principles, Policy & Practice,* 14(2), 171–184.

Hockett, J. A., & Doubet, K. J. (2013/2014). Turning on the lights: What pre-assessments can do. *Educational Leadership, 71*(4), 50–54. https://www.ascd.org/el/articles/turning-on-the-lights-what-pre-assessments-can-do

Ogle, D. M. (1986). K-W-L: A teaching model that develops active reading of expository text. *Reading Teacher, 39,* 564–570.

Providing Teacher Feedback to Students

What Is Teacher Feedback?

Feedback is information about a student's learning that helps the student take the next steps in the learning process. Feedback can come from many sources—teacher, peers, self, course materials, computers—and research shows students see teacher feedback as the most important. Teacher feedback is typically provided as a response to student work, whether from review of a formal assignment or from observation of the student's work in class. Effective feedback gives information to both teachers and students about where they stand relative to classroom learning goals and where they should go next. Effective feedback is based on the same success criteria students and teachers have been using during learning.

Why Is Teacher Feedback Important?

Formative teacher feedback is an important part of the formative learning cycle. Research routinely concludes that feedback is one of the most important factors affecting how much and how well students learn. However, research also shows that not all feedback is effective. The most effective feedback is, in general, elaborated (i.e., descriptive and explanatory comments, not grades or scores) and forward-looking, making at least one suggestion for improvement, and coupled with providing students the time to use the feedback. Interestingly, when students are asked what kinds of feedback they prefer, that's exactly what they ask for. Descriptive and explanatory comments can be delivered orally or as brief audio or video files (I have seen this done, e.g., in distance learning during the pandemic), handwritten on students' work, created with the comment function for word processed work, or in any other way that makes sense for supporting student follow-up.

How Do I Use Teacher Feedback in My Teaching and Assessment?

Feedback helps students navigate the formative learning cycle (Where am I going? Where am I now? Where to next?). The effectiveness of teacher feedback depends on the quality of the teacher's message, the student's receptivity and ability to use feedback, the content, and the classroom environment, among others. To maximize the likelihood that the feedback you give will in fact be useful to, and used by, students, it is helpful to use the metaphor of three lenses. A microscope lens looks at the details of something close-up—in this case, the feedback message. What feedback did you give, and how did you deliver it? A camera lens takes a snapshot of something—in this case, a snapshot of the learning that is happening in the feedback episode. What did you learn about student thinking from giving your feedback? What did the student learn about their learning from receiving it? A telescope lens looks at things that are far away—in this case, the ultimate effects of feedback. Did students have an opportunity to use the feedback? Did the feedback lead to increased learning or improved performance?

The Micro View: Looking at an Effective Feedback Message

Build feedback on the criteria for good work—criteria that indicate learning, not following directions—that you have already shared with students. I have often seen feedback that was overwhelmingly comprehensive—everything the teacher could think of that would improve the work. This kind of feedback is ineffective for a couple of reasons. First, it doesn't prioritize: what should the student focus on next? "Everything" feedback makes all next steps seem equal, and this is not true. Feedback should identify the next steps in a learning trajectory. Second, the sheer volume of feedback almost guarantees that students can't attend to all of it. Figure 4.1 lists recommendations for how to choose the words you use in your feedback and how to deliver them, in the form of do's and don'ts culled from research on

FIGURE 4.1
Recommendations for Feedback Messages and Their Delivery

Do	Don't
Focus on the work or the process the student used to do the work.	Focus on the student's personal characteristics.
Use shared criteria as the basis of your feedback (criterion-referenced). For struggling students, compare the student's work to your expectations for that student (self-referenced).	Compare the student's work to the work of other students (norm-referenced).
Describe the work.	Judge the work (e.g., "good" or "poor").
Describe strengths and phrase suggestions positively.	Belittle the student or the work.
Use clear language and check that the student understands it.	Obfuscate, mystify, muddle, or befuddle.
Give enough information to act on but not so much it overwhelms the student.	Overdo it, especially for students who are easily overwhelmed. Underdo it, especially for students who did well (everyone deserves to know what their teacher thought about their work).
Be timely, which is more about fitting into the formative learning cycle than being "quick" or "slow."	Give feedback after the opportunity to learn more is over.

feedback. Of course, no recommendation can cover all possible situations, so be thoughtful in your use of this list. In general, if your feedback contradicts one of the recommendations, you should be able to explain what about the situation contraindicates it.

As Figure 4.1 suggests, in your feedback, describe at least one thing the student did well and make at least one suggestion for improvement. Base what you suggest on what you know about the content and how the student learns it. What is the next thing, or couple things, that the student should focus on? Avoid feedback that tells the student everything that could possibly be improved. Avoid feedback that is so specific that all students would have to do is recopy what you wrote. The feedback should provide the appropriate level of scaffolding without doing the work for the student.

For example, we've all received feedback on written work that was more or less copyediting. All we had to do to make a perfect paper was, as a student once said, "Turn all of her red marks into black." The student doesn't really have to know why the teacher wanted those changes, though, so the revised work doesn't represent further learning. Instead, the teacher might put a dot or other agreed-upon mark next to the line(s) with an error, inviting the student to find it and fix it. For students who need a bit more scaffolding, the dot might be nearer the error, not in the margin. This technique works with identifying errors in worked math problems, as well. In responding to the feedback, students have to identify and deal with the error, in other words, move a little closer to their learning goal.

As you can see, when you make your "next steps" suggestions, you can use different amounts of scaffolding for different students' needs. *Reminder* prompts simply remind students of the learning target, for example, "Remember we're trying to find the length of the hypotenuse." *Scaffold* prompts ask detailed, focused questions or provide suggestions for steps to take, for example, "Can you find the square of each of the legs of the triangle? Can you add them together?" As the example in the previous paragraph showed, the scaffolding can be more or less intense depending on how small the steps are and how much the student is expected to do for each one. *Example* prompts literally give students an example, and in the case of our running example here that might mean showing a worked example of finding the hypotenuse of a right triangle when you have the length of the two legs. Figure 4.2 summarizes how to give feedback that feeds forward to different learners.

An important thing to remember when you're using Figure 4.2 is that you should evaluate success and struggle in terms of the specific learning target or goals you are assessing. Students who usually do well may struggle with certain concepts or skills, and students who usually struggle may be quite successful with some concepts or skills. Feedback is (or should be) goal specific. For successful and moderately successful students, and for students

FIGURE 4.2
How to Provide Feedback for Different Learners

For successful and moderately successful students
• Describe their work against shared criteria.
• Suggest at least one next step.
• Use *reminder* or *scaffold* prompts in your suggestions.
For students who struggle somewhat
• Describe their work against shared criteria.
• Suggest at least one next step.
• Use *scaffold* or *example* prompts in your suggestions.
For students who struggle a lot
• Describe their work in self-referenced terms.
• Reteach.

Note: Success and struggle refer to students' status with the learning targets you are assessing, not in general.

who struggle somewhat, the recommendations are similar, increasing the scaffolding for students who struggle. So, for a simple example of feedback on a descriptive paragraph, consider a prompt that asked students to write a paragraph describing what their lunchtime is like. Two students wrote that the cafeteria was very noisy and did not elaborate. For one student, your scaffold might be, "Can you write more about the noise in the cafeteria?" For another student who needs more scaffolding, you might combine that with an example prompt, saying "Can you write more about the noise in the cafeteria? For example, you might write, 'The bigger kids talk very loud and sometimes shout' and name some other noises you hear, too."

For students who struggle a lot, the recommendations are different. If the work is of such poor quality that describing it in criterion-referenced terms against a rubric, for example, would result in a failure experience, shift the reference. Describe the work in terms of the student's own past performance. If done carefully, this can avoid the failure experience. For example, if a student wrote a very poor paragraph this time but only wrote two sentences last time, you can say, "I see that you are learning to put more thoughts together in your paragraph, compared to last time. Now let's work on how those thoughts are related." If a student wrote the poor paragraph last time, but only two sentences this time, you can say, "I see you wrote two sentences. Remember you wrote that whole paragraph last time? Can you add to these two sentences to make your paragraph more complete?", perhaps adding an example prompt. And finally, feedback is commentary, not a shorthand lesson. If a student's work is simply nowhere near expectations, reteach. Don't try to stuff a whole lesson into a few feedback comments.

Research suggests students prefer feedback at the individual level, so that they can learn their personal strengths and improve their weaknesses. But small- or large-group feedback can work if there is something that a majority of the students need to practice or think about. Group feedback can, for example, come in the form of a minilesson: "Almost everyone forgot how to interpret the absolute value sign in these problems. Let's go over that again . . ."

The Snapshot View: Looking at an Episode of Learning

People often think about the information students get from teacher feedback. Less obvious, but just as important, is the information teachers get about students from a feedback episode. Teachers who look at student work for evidence of student thinking, not just correctness, can produce more targeted feedback than teachers who merely grade or score the work.

That information about student thinking is also useful for planning next instructional moves. Think of the opportunity for students to produce work, for you to review it and provide feedback, and for students to follow up by using the feedback as an episode of learning, part of the journey to the shared learning target or goal.

Several things will help you learn about student thinking during a feedback episode. First, for students to show their thinking, the assignment had to require that students do some thinking in the first place, not just recall facts. Use assignments that require students to analyze, synthesize, or create something. Then, when you look at students' work, try to infer what they must have been thinking in order to produce the work they did. Relate that information to the content in the learning goal. Identify what the next change in student thinking should be for the student to move closer to the goal. Focus the feedback you give the students on this understanding of their thinking and next steps. Use this information to plan your own next instructional steps, as well.

Several things will help students learn from feedback on their work. First, make sure students know the learning goal and success criteria. Share them during instruction and revisit them often, both before and during students' work. Then, base your observations of the work and the feedback you give on these learning goals and criteria. Check to make sure students understand your feedback and give students opportunities to ask questions. One way to do that is to have students explain to you or a peer what their feedback means and what they will do next. Then, give students an opportunity to improve their work. This is sometimes called closing the feedback loop.

Another thing that will help students learn from feedback is decoupling it from grades or other judgments. Students should be able to see feedback as information that will help them regulate their learning, moving closer to the goal. If students get feedback and a grade, research suggests most will focus on the grade. Give feedback on formative work done as part of instruction and practice. Then, when it's time for a grade, just grade—don't take the time to give descriptive feedback. And at every opportunity, help students see the connection between their formative practice work and the grade they end up with. Point this out explicitly. Of course, make sure the design of your instruction, formative assessment, and graded assessment are aligned with the learning goal so that this indeed happens.

The Long View: Looking at Feedback's Effects

The whole point of feedback is to help students move closer to the learning goal. The only way that can happen is if students do something with the feedback. Internal cognitive processing can be a next step (e.g., if a student finds out they are weak in an area and uses that information to shape their studying for a test), but typically a more active, in-class step is preferred. In no case is just sending feedback home so students will refer to it "next time" they do something similar sufficient. Learning just doesn't work that way. Students do not have file drawers of good advice for next time in their brains that they tap into at appropriate moments.

Students can use feedback in several ways. If the work was a complex performance, students can revise it, for example, doing another draft of a written assignment or modifying a project. If the work was a set of problems or other exercises with correct answers that the students will now know, students can show their improvement by studying their errors and doing a few additional, similar problems or exercises. In either case, students will also benefit from doing a brief reflection, either as a caption on their work or a brief oral chat with a partner, describing what they learned from using the feedback. In both cases, you should plan for that during class time. After using the feedback, students can reflect on what they learned.

In addition, you can take the long view by observing the effects of your feedback on students' subsequent work and understanding in further learning. For example, did the feedback you gave them on this writing assignment, coupled with their use of it to make their work better, result in better writing in the next writing assignment? Did the feedback you gave students on a set of math problems about solving equations with one variable, and their use of it to improve their understanding of that, help them in their subsequent work on equations in two variables, or did they make similar errors?

How Do I Involve Students in Teacher Feedback?

The most important thing you can do to involve students in teacher feedback is to give them opportunities to review the feedback, asking questions as needed, and then to use the feedback to improve. Sometimes feedback is provided on graded work more as an explanation of the grade—that is, backward-looking comments ("this is what you did")—or as forward-looking feedback intended for a general "next time you do something like this." As we have seen, this is not how feedback works; even the most dutiful student will not benefit much from general comments about "next time." Rather, make students part of a feedback conversation, where they interrogate your feedback, ask you questions to clarify anything that is fuzzy, and use the feedback while it is relevant and while they are still working on the learning goal.

Revision of work is the obvious next step. In the case of writing, next steps are built into the writing process (prewriting, planning, drafting, revising, editing, and publishing) that assume feedback at most if not all of those stages. Some of that feedback is teacher feedback. For any complex performance assessment, however, including not only written work but reports and projects of all sorts, the next steps often take the form of revision of the work, using the feedback. Sometimes, teachers ask students to note how they used the feedback and how it made the work better, using a sticky note or some other kind of paper or digital caption.

But revisions are only one way to take next steps. Teacher feedback on student work can also help students decide what concepts or skills they need to focus on to understand better or more deeply. These decisions can help students take next steps as they do additional work, including reading, preparing for tests, doing additional problems or exercises, and so on. This is less easy to see but no less important than revising student products. For example, if a teacher notices that a student is confusing the earth's rotation on its axis with its revolution around the sun, a student can review relevant resources (e.g., textbook, video) and look over previous work with an eye toward getting clear about the difference. This improvement in understanding may be reflected in future assignments or assessments.

Sometimes, teachers also involve students in feedback by asking them to note on an assignment, before they turn it in, what kind of feedback they would like to receive. This level of involvement turns on students and teachers using shared and mutually understood criteria. Without that, students don't have a clear idea of what to ask for. For example, if students are working on narrative writing and have learned that they can make characters come to life by what they say, what they do, and how the narrator describes them, a student who is having trouble with the first may ask for suggestions about how to use dialogue to help them characterize the protagonist in their story.

What Are Some Common Misconceptions About Feedback?

Probably the most common misconception is that grading provides useful feedback, or its corollary, that feedback is mostly a way to explain why a student received a certain grade. By the time an assignment is graded, it is often too late for feedback to be useful. In addition, knowing that some items were incorrect and some were correct does little to help students figure out what they understand and what they still need to work on. Although it is not strictly true that "grades are not feedback" (they are, of a sort), they are not feedback that feeds forward. Grades, by themselves, do not contain information that students can use to learn and improve. Elaborated feedback that describes students' current achievement and suggests immediate next steps is the type of feedback that research has found students want, need, and can use to improve.

FOR FURTHER READING

Brookhart, S. M. (2017). *How to give effective feedback to your students* (2nd ed.). ASCD.

Fisher, D., & Frey, N. (2009). Feed up, back, forward. *Educational Leadership, 67*(3), 20–25. https://www.ascd.org/el/articles/feed-up-back-forward

Hattie, J., & Clarke, S. (2019). *Visible learning: Feedback.* Routledge.

Housiaux, A., & Dickson, B. (2022). Less work, more learning: The promise of effective feedback. *Educational Leadership, 79*(9), 30–34. https://www.ascd.org/el/articles/less-work-more-learning-the-promise-of-effective-feedback

Ruiz-Primo, M. A., & Brookhart, S. M. (2018). *Using feedback to improve learning.* Routledge.

Smith, J. K., Lipnevich, A. A., & Guskey, T. R. (2023). *Instructional feedback: The power, the promise, the practice.* Corwin.

Wiggins, G. (2012). Seven keys to effective feedback. *Educational Leadership, 70*(1), 10–16. https://www.ascd.org/el/articles/seven-keys-to-effective-feedback

5

Helping Students Use Self- and Peer Assessment

What Are Self- and Peer Assessment?

Teachers are not the only source of feedback for students. Students themselves can be sources of feedback. Self-assessment happens when students compare the criteria for good work to their own work, identify their strengths and weaknesses accordingly, and decide what they think they should do next. Developing students who are capable of self-assessment is in some ways the goal of the formative learning cycle—indeed, a major goal of education in general. Peer assessment happens when peers compare the criteria for good work to a classmate's work, identify strengths, and make suggestions for improvement.

Both self- and peer assessment position students as the givers of feedback, but they serve slightly different purposes. Both are based on students reviewing work against the success criteria they have already been using during learning. Self-assessment helps students regulate their own learning and can, if done well, promote confidence and self-efficacy for learning and improve learning and performance. Peers who participate in peer assessment benefit from looking at others' examples. Applying success criteria to the work of others helps clarify those criteria for the peers who do it. If done well, peer assessment can also contribute to the building of a classroom learning community.

Why Are Self- and Peer Assessment Important?

Involving students in assessment is central to the formative enterprise. However, many studies of self- and peer assessment are actually studies of self- or peer grading. It is possible to get students and teachers to agree on a grade for a piece of work, but that doesn't really help with the learning process. Neither does research support self- or peer grading as a strategy for improving learning. However, when student self-assessment is used as part of the learning process, achievement does increase. Therefore, it is more productive to use self-assessment as a formative strategy and peer assessment as a collaborative learning strategy. This chapter will focus solely on these formative uses of self- and peer assessment and does not recommend self- and peer grading.

In addition, self- and peer assessment are both important because they involve students directly in assessment and—because they have to understand the criteria they are using and have at least some sense of what good work looks like—in progress toward a learning goal. In addition, self-assessment helps students develop self-efficacy and self-regulation skills that will stand them in good stead in school and out.

How Do I Use Self- and Peer Assessment in My Teaching and Assessment?

First and foremost, teachers can create the conditions in which effective self- and peer assessment are possible. Teachers who support self- and peer assessment do the following:

- Check for student understanding of the learning goal. Create (or cocreate with students), share, and clarify success criteria.
- Teach students how to apply criteria to examples of work, providing instruction, examples, and practice. As needed, provide scaffolding in the form of guidelines, rubrics, checklists, visual organizers, or feedback forms (paper or digital). For peer assessment, teach students to focus on the work, not the peer personally.
- Make expectations for the time and scope of a self- or peer assessment activity clear.
- Pay attention to the social and emotional aspects of peer assessment. In general, it is a good idea to pair similar-ability peers. Teach students the usefulness of constructive criticism, and be aware that some students may at first have trouble "criticizing" a peer.

- Give feedback on the quality of students' use of criteria as they review work (their own and others'). Monitor and coach students during self- and peer assessment.
- Teach students how to use feedback to improve their learning and performance, again using instruction, examples, and practice time. Give feedback to students on the quality of their use of feedback for improvement. As was the case for teacher feedback, if you're not going to provide time for the students to use their self- or peer feedback, don't bother making them do it.
- Provide enough time for students to use feedback (teacher, self-, and peer).
- Use self- and peer assessment formatively, not for grading.

As you and your students do these things, the quality of students' self- and peer assessment will improve. Of course, this is true about any learnable skill. Practice helps!

Self-Assessment

Figure 5.1 presents a list of different kinds of self-assessment strategies. With a climate of learning firmly in place, these strategies can work. Without, they will not. There is no magic in the strategies . . . the magic is in the

FIGURE 5.1
Strategies for Formative Student Self-Assessment

Purpose	Strategy	Examples
Self-assessment of amount of understanding	Students rate their perceived understanding with an indicator	Happy/sad faces Stand up/sit down Traffic lights Thumbs up/down/sideways Fist-to-five
Self-assessment of quality of understanding	Students describe their thinking in words	Reflective journals Quick-writes "Most clear" and "least clear" cards or worksheets One-minute papers Blank slides
Self-assessment of quality of work/performance	Rubric or checklist-based review of own work, with feedback	Rubrics and highlighters Visual organizers (e.g., "D.I.R.T." or "Rubric's Cube") Skills checklists Single-point rubrics

students' learning. For example, in a class where students experience being asked to respond as a quiz-like evaluation, and where they fear they will lose face if they are wrong, a "thumbs-up" strategy will not work. If you ask students in this class to rate their understanding, every thumb will be up, because no one will want to be the loser who doesn't understand. The same strategy, used in a class where students genuinely want to learn and realize that if they do, they will be rewarded with the satisfaction that learning brings and will perform well on graded assessments, can produce thoughtful responses of thumbs up, down, and sideways.

Note that some of the strategies in Figure 5.1 can be done as global reflections on one's understanding, and others require that specific criteria be used. For example, in the middle of a lesson on triangles, a teacher might ask students to indicate via thumbs how well they think they are understanding triangles. All of the formative self-assessment strategies for reviewing work or performance, however, require that students compare their work to criteria. Therefore, high-quality self-assessment requires high-quality criteria.

There are lots of ways to make illustrated, graphic-organizer-style worksheets for self- and peer assessment of all types, which can be very effective. Many of them are collected in the ASCD Action Tool *Formative Assessment Strategies for Every Classroom* (Brookhart, 2010). Others are available in Chappuis's (2019) *Seven Strategies of Assessment for Learning*, in other similar resources, or on the internet. The key to selecting a formatted aid for self- or peer assessment is to make sure it asks students to reflect on questions fit to the purpose for which you are using them. If it's not, for example, if it asks students to anticipate their grade, no matter how appealing the worksheet looks, don't use it.

Self-assessment of amount of understanding. Rather than assuming students are following during a lecture, demonstration, or problem set, why not ask? Students can rate their perceived understanding using a variety of gestures or indicators, most of which are probably familiar to you. Young children can use happy/sad face discs on their desk as teacher calls during their work, turning up a sad face if they need help or don't understand. You can survey a room of young children with a quick check, for example, "Stand up if you think you know what punctuation comes at the end of this sentence." Happy/sad faces and stand up/sit down are yes/no indicators. Traffic lights and thumbs up/down/sideways are three-level indicators (yes, maybe, no). Fist-to-five, where a fist means zero or "definitely no" and up to five fingers can be raised for increasing levels of certainty, gives a six-level indicator. Older students can handle this more nuanced judgment.

One thing all these indicator systems have in common is that they allow you to survey the entire class, not just a few students who are called on. The evidence can give you a sense of the whole classroom. Another thing these indicators have in common is that they are ratings of an *amount* of understanding or confidence in understanding. They don't indicate *what* students are understanding. For that, students need to use words and explain their thinking.

Self-assessment of quality of understanding. Students can explain their thinking in writing in reflective journals or quick-writes. Make sure the question you ask is the one about which you want students to self-assess. For example, in a lesson on floating and sinking, the questions "Explain why the cork floats in water" and "Describe something new you learned about floating today, and tell why it's interesting to you" will get different answers.

One-minute papers and various visual organizer worksheets about "most and least clear" ideas are more structured. Depending on the lesson, they may make effective exit tickets. Students get a bit of self-reflection at the end of a lesson and you (the teacher) get some information to think about as you plan the next lesson. For example, a one-minute paper may ask for "one thing I learned today" and "one question I have," and they are often formatted as half-page worksheets or digital forms. There are many variations, for example, a one-minute paper may ask for "three things I learned today," "two things I found interesting," and "one question I have." The last two are sometimes reversed (two things I still don't understand and one thing I want to know more about). The numbers, format, and questions can be adapted to fit students' age and developmental level.

You can build feedback breaks into any lesson to make sure students are taking time to self-assess and process the work or the reading they are doing or the lecture or video they are viewing. Simply pause at a good stopping place and use one of the self-assessments of amount of understanding. Written self-assessments may interrupt the flow of a lesson, but oral self-assessment of the quality of understanding can be done with a brief, well-facilitated class discussion about what students are thinking. Rob McEntarffer of Lincoln Public Schools uses a blank slide inserted into teacher presentation materials for secondary students at the point where he wants to ask them what they learned from the previous presentation and what questions they have. He found this was useful for both in-class and remote teaching.

Self-assessment of quality of work/performance. The previous self-assessments of amount or quality of understanding attempt to get "inside a kid's head" and elicit their perceptions of what they are thinking. For student work on an assignment, self-assessment should be based on shared criteria established before the work is begun, either by the teacher or by cocreating the criteria with the students. Although it is possible for students to do global, general self-assessment of their overall performance on assignments, it is not recommended, and this chapter does not discuss it.

That means that the first requirement for student self-assessment of their work is that they have criteria and that they use the criteria as they complete the work. All of the examples in Figure 5.1 for student self-assessment of the quality of their work are variations on applying the criteria to their own work.

If the criteria have been formatted as rubrics, students can use highlighters to annotate both their work and the rubric. For example, if they are learning to do persuasive writing, the rubrics might mention qualities like "states an opinion," "develops a logical argument," "supports the argument with details," and so on. Students might use a blue highlighter for "states an opinion" in the rubric and then the same blue to highlight the evidence—the place in their essay where they state their opinion. "Logical argument" might be yellow in the rubric and again at the places in the essay where they argue logically. Pink might be for "details," and so on. When the criteria and evidence are matched in that way, students can see if they are missing anything, and they can easily focus on each piece of evidence to evaluate its quality without being distracted by other bits of the essay.

Various visual organizers can help students put their self-assessment thoughts on paper. One that is currently making the rounds on the internet, in various formats, is called "D.I.R.T.", which means Dedicated Improvement and Reflection Time or some variation of that. It's simply a way to lay out students' analysis of their work and plans for revision, but the title lends a little fun. Similarly, Brookhart's (2010) "Rubric's Cube" lays out the performance level descriptions for each level of a rubric and the student's annotations about their own work in a visual that looks like a Rubik's Cube. Again, it's simply a way to lay out an analysis, but the metaphor adds a bit of fun.

If the criteria students are to use come in the form of a checklist, students can use a copy of their work and literally check (make a check or tick mark) next to each criterion, with a similar check on the place in their work that gives evidence of it, if the work is written. Single-point rubrics are a version of a checklist constructed with three columns. The criteria are listed in the center column. The columns to the left and right are left blank, for students to fill in. On the left the student can list "Concerns" or "Areas for Improvement." "Strengths" or "Areas of Excellence" are on the right.

Peer Assessment

Feedback from peer assessment should be provided for students to consider, and they should have the opportunity to use that feedback to revise or to respond with a reason why they are not taking a suggestion that is offered. Teach students that there should be no hard feelings about taking or leaving a peer's advice. Students are the authors of their own work. That said, the old adage "Two heads are better than one" is often true for peer assessment. Peers often have good ideas for improving work that the author didn't see.

Figure 5.2 presents a list of different kinds of peer assessment strategies. Of course, these are only strategies for assessing a peer's work or performance, not internal cognitive processes. Peers can only assess the evidence they can see. Again, the importance of using these in a learning-focused classroom rather than in a judgmental classroom atmosphere cannot be overstressed. Similarly, the quality of the criteria is important.

Written peer feedback. Many of the same strategies used for students' self-assessment of their work against criteria are also useful for peer assessment. Perkins (2003) developed the Ladder of Feedback that typically is presented as a ladder with four rungs, to remind students to do four things, in order: (1) Clarify—ask questions about the work, (2) Value—comment on the work's strengths, (3) Concerns—comment on your concerns about the work, and (4) Suggest—make suggestions for improvement. Although it would be possible to use the Ladder of Feedback strategy without explicit reference to criteria, the feedback will be better if criteria are used. Criteria

FIGURE 5.2
Strategies for Peer Assessment and Collaborative Learning

Purpose	Strategy	Examples
Peer assessment of quality of work/performance	Review of peer's work, with narrative feedback based on criteria	• Ladder of feedback • Rubrics and highlighters
	Review of peer's work, with feedback based on criteria and structured feedback with a visual organizer	• Two stars and a wish • Stars and steps (or stars and stairs) • Glow and grow • Plus-delta • Single-point rubrics
	Review of peer's work, with feedback based on criteria and dialogue between peers	• What do you think? What do I think? • Elbow partner switch • Peer conferencing forms • Peer response forms

focus student comments on aspects of the work that have been identified as important for students making progress toward their learning goal.

Other written forms of feedback against criteria used for self-assessment, such as the Rubrics and Highlighters strategy, can also be used for peer assessment. Sometimes, it is helpful to scaffold peer feedback with a structured feedback form. These often take the form of a visual organizer.

Peer feedback scaffolded with a feedback form. Again, many of the same formats used to scaffold self-assessment can also be used for peer assessment. Single-point rubrics, for example, can be used that way.

A number of metaphors have been made into peer feedback forms that oblige the peer to make comments about what was done well and suggestions for improvement. These are sometimes illustrated and printed on half-sheets for easy use, built into digital forms, or even drawn on sticky notes that can be affixed to the paper they are commenting on. There are many versions, for example, two stars and a wish, stars and steps (or stars and stairs), glow and grow, or plus/delta for older students. Many different ways of illustrating these have been designed, each of which uses a simple two-category framework or sometimes a T-chart.

Peer feedback with dialogue between peers. Peer feedback without follow-up dialogue between the peers is in some ways a missed opportunity. Any of the previously described peer feedback strategies can be followed by a brief discussion where peers review their feedback with each other. This may be as simple as an elbow partner switch, where two students switch papers, each giving peer feedback, and then switch back for a brief discussion. To scaffold this work, various forms have been developed. For example, Brookhart (2010) has a simple two-columned "What do you think? What do I think?" form designed for independent review of the same work and then a discussion. Chappuis (2015) shows examples of a peer conferencing form and a peer response form.

How Do I Involve Students in Self- and Peer Assessment?

This question is a bit redundant in a chapter on self- and peer assessment, which by definition involve students. However, the question gives us an opportunity to think about quality involvement and expand a bit on the bullet points in the "how to" section. Certainly, as for any activity assigned in a classroom, it is possible for students to move in a perfunctory way through a self- or peer assessment session. What are some ways to help students want to participate enthusiastically in, and gain from, student-involved assessment?

First, create a climate of learning in the classroom. Use learning-focused language when you speak with students. Accept and encourage student thinking, and cultivate the understanding that mistakes are necessary for learning.

Second, share learning targets or goals and criteria with students in a form they can use. Develop the criteria with students when possible, for example by analyzing exemplary work. Check to make sure students understand the criteria before asking them to assess their own or peers' work.

Third, teach students how to apply criteria to their own or others' work. This analytical task does not come naturally and requires instruction. Model it for students, showing how for each criterion they need to look for evidence in the work. Give students feedback on the quality of their self- or peer assessment.

Fourth, make it fun. Student self- or peer assessment should result in feelings of self-improvement and the satisfaction of working together on something important. Self- and peer assessment sessions should lead directly to improved work and student satisfaction that are palpable. Be explicit about this with your students ("I'm so glad we took the time to look over these paragraphs. The next drafts are so much more interesting to read").

Hattie and Clarke (2019, p. 12) sum up this approach to quality involvement of students in their own assessment by saying that students need to bring "skill, will, and thrill" to their involvement in assessment. They need some skills, which can be taught, for example, understanding what criteria they will be looking for and how to apply them. They need the will or disposition to believe that the self- or peer assessment will be helpful and worthwhile. They need the thrill or motivation to participate in the exercise and get as much as they can out of it. The process should be fun.

What Are Some Common Misconceptions About Self- and Peer Assessment?

One common misconception is that self- and peer assessment mean self- or peer grading. As the introduction to this chapter showed, productive self- and peer assessments are formative actions. They happen during learning, and their purpose is to advance learning.

Perhaps a more troubling misconception is that a form—for example, a nicely illustrated student-friendly rubric with lines beside it for comments—is all that is needed for self- or peer assessment. This is not true. Self- and peer assessment are cognitive activities at the highest level. In Bloom's taxonomy terms, these assessment activities require analysis, matching stated criteria to evidence in a piece of work, and evaluation, judging how well the evidence stands up to the criteria. This chapter has stressed that students need to be taught how to do this, with appropriate scaffolding, coaching, and feedback. Although doing these things well is not for the faint of heart, the rewards, in terms of creating a classroom climate of learning and increasing student achievement and academic self-efficacy, are well worth it. Plus, when well-managed, there are social and emotional benefits to creating students who can assess their own work and who can give and receive peer feedback.

FOR FURTHER READING

Andrade, H. (2013). *Student-centered assessment video suite.* https://studentsatthecenterhub.org/resource/student-centered-assessment-video-suite/

Andrade, H., & Valtcheva, A. (2009). Promoting learning and achievement through self-assessment. *Theory into Practice, 48*(1), 12–19.

Brookhart, S. M. (2010). *Formative assessment strategies for every classroom: An ASCD action tool* (2nd ed.). ASCD.

Chappuis, J. (2015). *Seven strategies of assessment for learning* (2nd ed.). Pearson.

Frey, N., Hattie, J., & Fisher, D. (2018). *Developing assessment-capable visible learners, grades K–12.* Corwin.

Gregory, K., Cameron, C., & Davies, A. (2011). *Self-assessment and goal setting* (2nd ed.). Connections Publishing.

Hattie, J., & Clarke, S. (2019). *Visible learning: Feedback.* Routledge.

Moss, C. M., & Brookhart, S. M. (2019). *Advancing formative assessment in every classroom* (2nd ed.). ASCD.

Perkins, D. (2003). *King Arthur's round table: How collaborative conversations create smart organizations.* John Wiley and Sons.

Sackstein, S. (2017). *Peer feedback in the classroom: Empowering students to be the experts.* ASCD.

Topping, K. (2009). Peer assessment. *Theory into Practice, 48*(1), 20–27.

6

Extending Student Thinking with Questioning Strategies

What Are Questioning Strategies?

The questioning strategies discussed in this chapter are ways to address questions to students for instruction- and assessment-related purposes. These can include encouraging student thinking, checking for understanding, reviewing previous content, stimulating an active discussion, enabling students to express their thoughts and feelings, and more, but one thing they have in common is that the student responses, once voiced, become available to other students and the teacher. That is, student responses become evidence of student thinking, and when they do, they become a means of formative assessment. The questioning strategies discussed in this chapter are all intended for formative assessment. For recommendations about writing test questions for summative assessment, see Chapters 15 and 16. Of course, there are some aspects of questioning that are common to both, but this chapter focuses on questioning strategies for extending student thinking to serve formative assessment and stimulate further learning.

Why Are Questioning Strategies Important?

Strategic use of questions promotes formative classroom discourse. Formative classroom discourse, where students talk with each other and not just to the teacher, can provide a safe space for students to question their own and others' ideas, develop new ideas or extend developing ideas, and self-assess. Formative classroom discourse based on strategic questioning also helps students focus on important learning targets and success criteria.

In most school classrooms, there is a lot of teacher talk. A conventional pattern is the initiate-respond-evaluate (IRE) structure. The teacher asks a question, calls on a student to respond, evaluates the answer, and moves on. Sadly, this pattern is still common today. It positions the teacher as the arbiter of knowledge and implies to students that learning means getting questions right when the teacher asks them. Further, this pattern has twice as much teacher talk (initiating and evaluating) as student talk (responding). The strategies in this chapter aim to support a different discourse pattern, where student talk is central and discussion, not oral quizzing, occurs. As a colleague of mine once remarked, "The ones who are doing the talking are the ones who are doing the learning."

How Do I Use Questioning Strategies in My Teaching and Assessment?

What you and your students learn from their responses to questions is largely dependent on the questions that are asked. To get evidence of how students are thinking, ask questions that require students to think. To get evidence of students' thinking about a specific learning target or goal, match questions to that goal. Seems obvious, but it is easy for a classroom discussion to become a missed opportunity because questions are on topic but not a precise match to intended learning goals or student thinking. Figure 6.1 summarizes strategies for questioning for formative assessment.

Match Questions to Instructional and Assessment Purpose

Teachers who do this well understand their learning goals and what it takes to achieve them at a deep level. In addition, they understand different kinds of questions and use them strategically.

One way to categorize questions is whether they are open or closed. *Open questions* have more than one good answer. Open questions are not necessarily difficult ("Why do you think the Cat came to visit Sally and her brother on their cold, wet day at home?"). But they allow for multiple answers, and students can find a way in from many different levels (e.g., "He wanted to" or "The Cat was trying to help the children not be bored" or "The Cat was in the children's imagination as they helped themselves not be bored"—all of which could lead to productive discussion about *The Cat in the Hat*). They almost always require higher-order thinking of some sort

FIGURE 6.1
Questioning Strategies for Formative Classroom Discourse

Purpose	Strategy	Examples
Match questions to instructional and assessment purpose.	Understand different kinds of questions, and use them strategically.	• Open vs. closed questions • Questions with multiple "ways in" • Recall, observation, or thought questions
Give students time to give thoughtful responses.	Use wait time.	• Think time/no hands up • Pair or square thinking
Extend student thinking and discussion.	Ask follow-up questions and other productive talk moves after students' initial responses.	• Invite elaboration (e.g., agree/disagree/add) • Check for understanding • Revoice • Ask students to explain their reasoning
Sequence questions purposefully.	Plan a series of two or more questions that develop and give evidence of student thinking.	• Extending and lifting • Broad to narrow or narrow to broad • Circular path from a main point and back
Help students ask effective questions.	Scaffold students' questions to help them develop knowledge and skill in questioning.	• Question starters • Questioning quads
Base discussion on students' ideas.	Ask questions based on what students are thinking about.	• Reflective toss
Ensure that every student has an opportunity to speak.	Call on students randomly, sometimes called "cold calling," in a safe and accepting environment.	• Popsicle sticks • Random numbers

(typically, questions that require students to analyze, evaluate, or create knowledge). *Closed questions,* in contrast, have one right answer or sometimes a set of right answers (e.g., all real numbers greater than seven). Use open questions to assess students' thinking and closed questions to assess students' recall of facts, concepts, or solutions to right-answer problems (typically, questions that require students to remember, understand, or apply knowledge). Most students prefer open questions, and open questions garner more student responses than closed questions.

Don't confuse open and closed questions with broad and narrow questions. Open questions can be narrow, like the question about the Cat's appearance; somewhat broad (e.g., "What kinds of things do children do when they are bored?"); or broader (e.g., "How can we help children be safe at home?"). The section on sequencing says more about narrow and broad questions.

Both closed and open questions are appropriate sometimes. However, research suggests that when teachers just ask questions on the fly, they ask a disproportionate number of closed questions, and students don't have the opportunity to think. Further, too many closed questions can come across to students as an oral quiz, with the teacher checking to see who has memorized some right answers. This will work against developing a classroom climate of learning. A few closed questions may be useful for orienting students to what the discussion will be about (e.g., "Who is the main character in *The Cat in the Hat*?"), but for extending student thinking, use open questions.

Another way to categorize questions is according to whether the answer requires recall, observation, or thought. Questions shift with students' developmental level and with familiarity with the content. For example, "What is six plus four?" is a recall question for most older students, but it may be an observation question for younger ones (e.g., involving counting discs).

In any case, the "right" question to ask is the one that will have students contemplating the content they are learning using the kind of thinking they are meant to be learning. No matter how clever a question sounds, if it doesn't do that, it's not the right one to use. Prepare questions ahead of time; good open questions that are a spot-on match with learning targets take time and thought to design. Use these questions to support formative classroom discourse—where students learn by having the discussion and where everyone gets evidence about that learning. Ask a question, and then give students time to think.

Give Students Time to Give Thoughtful Responses

Use wait time, which probably should be called "think time." Give students time to think after you ask a question; in addition, give students time to think after one student has spoken, before another responds. Teach students to use that time to reflect on what has been said first, and then how they might respond.

If you just wait after you ask a question, some students may simply do nothing. To help students actively process what they have just heard and think constructively about what they might contribute, structure "think time/no hands up" where students know specifically that they should first think about the question that was just posed (or, in discussion, the student contribution they just heard) and then about how they might respond. Then let students know when you are ready for them to volunteer to contribute, if you are taking volunteers, or use a strategy for random calling.

Another very useful way to structure wait time is to have students process their thoughts aloud by talking with a peer. Think-Pair-Share is the classic of this type (Lyman, 1981). Ask a question, give students a minute or two of individual think time, then have them turn to a partner and share thoughts. Finally, have them share with the whole class by calling randomly on several pairs to summarize their conversation or calling on several individuals to report on what their partner thought. Sometimes, teachers have students write or draw their thoughts before they share. This strategy has several advantages. Students get a chance to process their thoughts before they speak to the whole class, and by the time they do, they have something to say. Everyone in the class has a chance to think, not just the students who end up called on. Finally, the strategy teaches students that it's a good idea to think before you speak.

A variation of this strategy is "square thinking." The teacher asks a question, students think with a partner first, and then two pairs of partners join together to share their thoughts in a four-student group.

It is also useful to develop norms for students participating in discussion. For example, students can be taught to do the following: talk with each other, not the teacher; share their thoughts and explain their thinking; ask questions when they don't understand something; take responsibility for not talking too much; encourage students who may be reticent. Teaching students how to listen is important, too.

Extend Student Thinking and Discussion

After a student answers a question, invite other students to elaborate, using one of these talk moves:

- A simple strategy is to ask students if they agree, disagree, or have something to add to what was just said. In time, students learn to do this themselves.
- Check for understanding of what was just said, for example by asking someone to put what was said in their own words.
- Repeat what the student just said in your own words and ask the student to confirm or disconfirm that you heard correctly. This is sometimes called revoicing.
- Ask students to explain their reasoning. For example, you can ask why, or ask for the evidence they used to arrive at a conclusion, or simply ask them to "say more."

Sequence Questions Purposefully

Plan a series of questions that lead a discussion in a purposeful direction. One type of series extends and lifts the discussion from simple observations to more insightful or deeper inferences. Marzano and Simms (2014) describe this type of sequence as asking students questions about (1) details, (2) the categories the details exemplify, (3) elaboration on their previous answers, and (4) evidence for their elaborations. Other questioning sequences exist, as well (Brown & Wragg, 1993). Questioning sequences from narrow to broad support student thinking about gathering knowledge, applying it narrowly, and then applying it more broadly. For example, students might discuss specific things they have learned about the climate in their region and eventually answer questions about climate change more globally. The opposite sequence (broad to narrow) works for some learning goals, for example, applying a general principle from history to a specific issue in current events. Another pattern, a circular discussion, helps students deal with a key point, explore related issues, and return to the key point.

Help Students Ask Effective Questions

Students who can ask effective questions have an important tool they can use to increase their learning and make progress toward their learning goals. Question starters—question stems or templates that students can use to construct questions—help scaffold students' learning how to do that. Make sure the question starters are appropriate to the purpose of the questions. For example, if you want students to predict or make inferences, question starters like "If we changed ___, what do you think would (or would not) happen? Why?" would be useful. If you want students to organize material or discover relationships, question starters like "How are ___ and ___ alike (or different)?" would be useful.

Teachers can use question starters in many different individual or group activities. For example, Questioning Quads is a strategy for generating questions from texts. Put students in groups of four. Designate the four roles: questioner, paraphraser, responder, and feedback giver. Give each group a pile of appropriate question starters or a list on a tablet or device. Assign a text to be read silently. Then, the questioner chooses a question starter at random and asks a question based on the text. The paraphraser puts that question into his or her own words. The responder answers the question. The feedback giver summarizes what the group learned. Roles rotate and the process repeats until students understand the text.

Base Discussion on Students' Ideas

Questions that respond to student ideas help engage students in active thinking. An example of such a strategy is the *reflective toss* (van Zee &

Minstrell, 1997), whose name is a sports metaphor. The reflective toss inverts the IRE sequence. Instead of starting with a teacher question, Minstrell recommended "catching" the meaning of a student's prior statement and "throwing" responsibility for thinking about it back to the student. So instead of the teacher initiating a question, followed by a student response and a teacher evaluation, the sequence is student statement, teacher question, and another student statement. When a student makes a statement, whether in answer to a teacher or peer question or just in the context of discussion, identify ("catch") the main point the student is making and ask the student a clarifying question ("throw") about it. This allows the student to extend his own thinking, and then offers the possibility of bringing others in, too.

Ensure That Every Student Has an Opportunity to Speak

Randomized calling strategies accomplish this goal by using popsicle sticks with students' names on them, or numbers for table and seat, or even a random number generator (this works well in a high school math class). "Cold calling," as randomizing is sometimes called, only works if the students perceive the environment is safe and no one will punish or belittle them for poor answers, so take stock of your classroom environment before you try it. The argument in favor of it is that every student deserves a chance to think and speak—and thereby learn—not just students who are quick to raise their hands. Make cold calling part of classroom routines, for example, during an introductory or debriefing discussion, to normalize and regularize it.

Ask the question first, before you call on a student, when all students still have a chance of being selected. If you begin by selecting the student, and your question starts, for example, "Mara, what are some different ways students learn about current events in the news?"—anyone who isn't Mara can simply stop listening. This strategy of question first, then calling on a student, is appropriate for both cold calling and calling on volunteers.

How Do I Involve Students in Questioning?

Students are already involved in questioning and classroom discourse. The trick is to help students feel heard. Listen to what students express, about both content and their own thoughts and feelings, take them seriously, and respond to them with respect.

Questioning also lends itself to some fun activities. For example, one reading teacher I know gave students a printed template for a cube. Students were to read a text and ask six questions, printing one on each part of the template that would end up being a side of the cube. The teacher specified what kinds of questions she wanted the students to ask, so there was a mixture of factual and inferential questions. Students cut out their templates and glued them to form cubes, which they then rolled like dice. Partners had to answer the question that appeared on the top of the cube when it came to rest.

What Are Some Common Misconceptions About Questioning?

One common misconception about questioning is that its primary purpose is to evaluate what students already know. As this chapter has shown, that encourages a "quiz" mindset and works against the power of questions to stimulate students' thinking and help them express their ideas.

Another misconception is that questioning "comes naturally" to teachers as they are teaching lessons. If this were true, it would not be the case that most teachers ask primarily simple recall questions. Effective questions need to be prepared ahead of time, keeping in mind their particular purpose in the lesson, their relationship to the learning goal, and anticipated student responses.

FOR FURTHER READING

Brown, G., & Wragg, E. C. (1993). *Questioning*. Routledge.

Fisher, D., Frey, N., Anderson, H., & Thayre, M. (2015). *Text-dependent questions, grades K–5: Pathways to close and critical reading*. Corwin.

Fisher, D., Frey, N., & Rothenberg, C. (2008). *Content-area conversations: How to plan discussion-based lessons for diverse language learners*. ASCD.

Kay, M. R. (2022). Listen up! A strategy for student discussions. *Educational Leadership, 79*(6). https://www.ascd.org/el/articles/listen-up-a-strategy-for-student-discussions

Lyman, F. T. (1981). The responsive classroom discussion: The inclusion of all students. In A. Anderson (Ed.), *Mainstreaming digest* (pp. 109–113). University of Maryland Press.

Marzano, R. J., & Simms, J. A. (2014). *Questioning sequences in the classroom*. Marzano Research Laboratories.

Michaels, S., Shouse, A., & Schweingruber, H. (2008). *Ready, set, science!* National Academies Press.

Moss, C. M., & Brookhart, S. M. (2019). *Advancing formative assessment in every classroom* (2nd ed.). ASCD.

Small, M. (2012). *Good questions: Great ways to differentiate mathematics instruction* (2nd ed.). Teachers College Press.

van Zee, E., & Minstrell, J. (1997). Using questioning to guide student thinking. *Journal of the Learning Sciences, 6*(2), 227–269.

Walsh, J. A. (2022). *Questioning for formative feedback: Meaningful dialogue to improve learning.* ASCD.

Walsh, J. A., & Sattes, B. (2015). *Questioning for classroom discussion: Purposeful speaking, engaged listening, deep thinking.* ASCD.

7

Considering Homework as Assessment

What Is Homework?

"Homework" is an all-purpose word these days, having moved from school to general vocabulary ("Do your homework before you go on a trip"). It began in the context of the rote learning and recitation methods used in schools of yesteryear. Memorizing spelling words or math facts, for example, can be done at home. So originally, homework meant assignments for children to continue at home the rote tasks they were doing in school. The pro- and anti-homework pendulum has swung several times since then, often related to current events or the views of popular leaders. Over the years, homework has expanded to include all manner of independent work, and some consider it a mark of "rigorous" teaching. In this chapter, "homework" means academic work students are assigned to do at home and bring (or send, in the case of digital files) back to class.

Why Is Homework Important?

Homework is best understood as an opportunity for practice and formative assessment. Students benefit most when homework reviews material that they have not yet mastered (and therefore need to practice) but that they are able to work on independently. Considering homework as part of the formative learning cycle implies that, except in unusual circumstances, it should not be graded (or checked for completion without looking at its contents) but rather be used as an opportunity for some sort of feedback about where students are now and where they should go next. The next section suggests ways to do this. Other activities that sometimes are called "homework," for example, bringing egg cartons to school for a craft project, should be called something else, such as helping with supplies.

How Do I Use Homework in My Teaching and Assessment?

The basic methods for using homework as part of the formative learning cycle are very similar to the methods for using other formative assessment strategies. First, be intentional about the purpose of the homework assignment. That purpose should fit within the current learning cycles, both for short-term daily learning targets and the longer-term learning goals they feed. Second, make sure the homework is a high-quality task that matches the intended purpose. Design homework to be differentiated or personalized as needed and to give effective practice. Third, provide students feedback on their homework, and do not grade it. Fourth, use the results. As for any formative assessment strategy, for homework to be worthwhile it needs to feed students' learning forward. Students need opportunities to reflect on their homework feedback and use it in further work. Teachers can use homework as an opportunity to get more formative information upon which to base instructional follow-up. Figure 7.1 summarizes strategies for designing and using homework as formative assessment.

Set the Purpose for Homework

Vatterott (2018, p. 104) suggests five possible purposes for homework: pre-learning, diagnosis (or pre-assessment, as this is called in Chapter 3), checking for understanding, practice at the application level, and processing (reflection, application, analysis, synthesis). For homework to function as formative assessment, one of these purposes needs to fit into a formative learning cycle, that is, it needs to coordinate with what students are aiming to learn, either for a short-term learning target or a longer-term learning goal.

Traditional pre-learning homework, for example, reading a chapter in a textbook and answering some chapter questions, is not very formative because it engages students in learning by themselves, without necessarily setting a learning goal. More effective is homework that draws students' attention to an upcoming learning goal, generates some interest,

FIGURE 7.1
Strategies for Using Homework as Formative Assessment

Purpose	Strategies	Example
Set the purpose for homework	• Pre-learning and pre-assessment • Checking for understanding • Practice at the application level • Processing and reflecting	A 10th grade history teacher uses a homework assignment for pre-learning about the American Revolution.
Use high-quality tasks and design strategies for homework	• Build students' mastery and autonomy over their learning • Feature application of skills • Use brief tasks that leverage self-regulation over rote practicing of errors • Use tasks that are developmentally appropriate • Present a moderate level of challenge • Differentiate tasks	Students skim the chapter and select one section to read, based on their interest. They prepare three "thinking" questions based on the section they read. Questions may not be simple questions of fact and may not be the same as the end-of-chapter textbook questions. The next day, in groups, students discuss their questions as part of their introduction to the topic.
Provide feedback for homework	• Teacher feedback to whole class • Teacher feedback to individuals • Feedback from self or peers	Teacher uses the information she hears to tweak her instructional plans for the unit.
Use the results of homework	• Provide feedback and choose next instructional moves, including both content and pacing • Student in-class revision, reflection, or further practice	

and provides some pre-assessment information about what students already know. For example, students might be asked to draw a family tree in preparation for a unit about the family and culture.

Checking for understanding is an underused type of method with great formative potential. Instead of assigning students a problem set for practice, for example, consider asking students to do two or three problems and explain their work. This allows the teacher to check whether students understand the kind of problem and the reasoning behind it. It also, importantly, avoids having students do a large number of practice problems incorrectly, developing habits that will need to be unlearned, which is very difficult. Checking for understanding homework is possible in almost all subject areas. In language arts, students studying characterization can identify places in a short story where a given character said or did something that was key to understanding their character, to check that they understand how characters are developed. In science, students can answer questions about experiments or phenomena that show their understanding. In history, students can answer questions about persons or events that show their understanding. The questions can be brief and prepared as an entrance ticket for the next class, and follow-up should ensue in the form of a discussion or group work or something that will allow the students to use their thinking.

Give homework to help students practice a skill after you have checked and are sure they understand how to do the skill. For students who don't, "practice" homework is new learning, and homework is not a good place for that. Students may end up practicing incorrectly or developing misconceptions. So always make sure you assign practice homework that truly is practice. Also, small amounts of practice spaced over time (distributed practice) is more effective for learning than a larger amount of practice done in one sitting (massed practice). Third, as always, to use practice homework formatively, students must receive feedback on it and an opportunity to use the feedback, for example, on the day that it is due. Without this important follow-up, practice homework does not help students with the formative learning cycle.

Homework can involve more complex thinking or reflection in a content area. Simple reflection about one's work on a few problems can be very helpful for short-term learning goals. For older students especially, some complex assignments can mirror the kind of work they are learning to do; for example, students of history learn to write papers on people or events. For this complex work to contribute to students' learning, it must be closely coupled with daily and long-term learning targets, and students should know what it is they are trying to learn. Also, the out-of-class portion of the assignment should be tethered to in-class checkpoints, so that students have a chance to articulate what it is they are learning by doing the assignment, what questions it is raising, and why what they are finding or constructing is important or interesting.

A homey counterexample can help make this point. I remember a middle school "term paper" assignment where each student was allowed to choose a topic, do library research, and write a paper, without any guidance except final format requirements and the library skills that had been taught in general—and given four weeks to do it! Nothing relating to the paper happened in class in the four weeks between the assignment and its collection, or at least, if it did it was lost on me. Dutiful students like myself probably learned some things about the content they read about and about the experience of looking for information in a library, but many students may have missed even those simple goals. Important points were missed; for example, I did not learn that effective term papers were based on research questions, not just topics, until many years later.

If teachers assign a complex, long-term assignment, they need to clearly communicate what students will learn by doing the assignment, what criteria they and the students will use in evaluating the work, and why this learning is important. Further, they should design checkpoints along the way in class that match with important daily and long-term learning goals, to help students get feedback along the way about what they are learning as they do the work. Finally, teachers should make sure that any long-term assignment is equitable for all the learners in the classroom. These design considerations lead us into the next section.

Use High-Quality Tasks and Design Strategies for Homework

A high-quality homework task is one that is effective for its purpose and actively involves students in the pursuit of a learning goal. A high-quality homework task builds students' sense of mastery and autonomy over the material—which is why incorporating student choice into homework tasks is a good idea. A high-quality homework task uses student time and focus effectively and does not require students to spend time on irrelevant skills—for example, creating a presentation that teaches students a lot about how to use PowerPoint but only requires copying and pasting information about the topic. A high-quality homework task features application of knowledge rather than memorization. A high-quality homework task yields formative assessment information that both students and teachers can use for future learning. For example, instead of asking students to do a set of 15 fraction problems, give students the problem set and ask them to identify the two problems they think will be most difficult for them to solve, solve them, and then explain in words what seemed like it would be difficult, how they solved the problem, and what they learned by doing so.

Well-designed homework should be brief, designed with students' developmental level in mind, and differentiated. Regarding brevity, remember that small amounts of distributed practice repeated over time are more effective for learning than large amounts. Regarding developmental level, homework is not recommended at all for primary students. In upper elementary school, a small amount of homework may be effective at helping students begin to learn the regulatory skills required for future years. In middle and high school, more, but still not overwhelming, amounts of well-designed homework may be useful.

Homework should be pitched at a moderate level of challenge—not so difficult as to be frustrating and not so easy as to be worthless. There are several ways to differentiate homework. One is to give different assignments of different difficulty levels, to the extent that the learning goal allows. For example, two-step word problems requiring students to use multiplication and addition can be created with larger and smaller numbers, making the calculations easier or more difficult but still reviewing solving two-step word problems with two operations.

Another differentiation strategy is to assign a problem set or other task and a time. For example, you might tell students to spend 20 minutes on a set of problems. Some will do more than others in that time, but from each you will get information about students' understanding.

Yet another differentiation strategy is to use more and less scaffolding. For example, some students may be asked to read and reflect on a section of expository text, using reflection questions. The same assignment may be broken down into smaller steps for some students, who may read smaller chunks of text at a time and answer a brief question after each chunk, or perhaps using prepared sentences with blanks to fill in or choices to circle for their reflection. Some students may use a graphic organizer instead. The criterion for selecting a differentiation method is whether the timing, scaffolding, or another method would allow students to show what they know, in a way that would help them approach the learning goal.

For homework tasks requiring rote memory, consider letting students choose their practice method. For example, to learn math facts they may use flash cards, writing the facts, using counters, playing a quiz game, or something else. Students can be assigned to practice something specific (e.g., the 6 and 7 times tables) but given a choice of how to do it. They can come to class ready to both recite the math facts and explain how their learning strategy helped them (or not). In pairs the next day, students can practice using a partner's strategy, and compare their experiences and preferences for different kinds of studying.

Provide Feedback for Homework

A key aspect of considering homework as formative assessment is making sure that students get feedback on their homework and a chance to use the feedback to improve. Teachers can give quick feedback to the whole class or to students individually, or they can facilitate a feedback activity like "My Favorite No" (see Chapter 1). Students can give feedback using self- or peer assessment (see Chapter 5), for example, using the partner study strategy explained in the previous section.

The importance of feedback on homework cannot be overstated because it is feedback that will propel the student forward. Effective feedback helps clarify the learning goal for students (Where am I going?) and helps them figure out Where am I now? and Where to next?

A corollary of providing feedback is that homework should *not* be graded. Formative work loses much of its informational and motivational value if it also carries an evaluation. Many students will pay attention to the grade and disregard other, more actionable, feedback. Research suggests students actually prefer feedback to grades, anyway, and students can be taught that the feedback that helps them improve will, ultimately, help them receive grades that reflect that learning.

Use the Results of Homework

Not grading homework does *not* mean not looking at it! No student will do (for long) work that seems to be ignored or doesn't make a difference. Teachers can use the information about student learning that is in homework for providing feedback, for designing follow-up instruction and future assignments, and for decisions about the timing and pacing of future work. Students can use the results of homework in class activities designed to follow up on the homework, in reflection on their learning or revision of work, and in future studying.

How Do I Involve Students in Homework?

Of course, students are involved in homework by definition—they're the ones who have to do it. However, strategies that involve students in choosing strategies and tasks for their homework and in generating and using formative assessment information to help them learn make homework more formative and more student-involved. Consider this difference. Two classes are working on the learning goal of doing multistep problems with two or more operations. One class is assigned 10 such problems for homework. Another class is given the set of 10 problems and asked to do the first two, write an explanation of their process for one of them, and decide how many of the remaining eight problems they need to do to get ready for a class activity solving similar problems the next day. The first class gets practice with multistep problems (assuming they were doing them correctly). The second class gets practice with multistep problems and practice regulating their learning toward the goal of doing multistep problems with two or more operations. That is, the second class is learning math and also learning how to learn math.

What Are Some Common Misconceptions About Homework?

One common misconception about homework is that lots of homework, especially lots of difficult homework, is the hallmark of a rigorous education. In fact, a small amount of homework at an appropriate level of challenge is the hallmark of a rigorous education. This chapter has described such homework from the point of view of the students. It is worth considering the teacher point of view, as well. Anyone can make up long sheets of hard problems or assign tough reading without much scaffolding, and this is certainly not the hallmark of a meticulous teacher. Only teachers who pay attention to formative assessment information, who know where their students are and what they need next, can provide precisely the right homework for the moment—and thus truly rigorous teaching.

A second misconception has to do with parental help with homework. Some think parents should not help their children and that to do so is cheating. Others think that getting homework "right" is so important that parents can even do homework for their children. Both extremes are misconceptions. The best help that parents or guardians can provide for their children is to scaffold the self-regulation skills that allow children to succeed with homework. They can ask their children what homework they have, how they plan to do it, and what they need to accomplish it. They can provide coaching and clues about timing and prioritizing, for example, suggesting that doing the "hardest" (to that student) homework first might be wise, saving easier homework for later when the child begins to tire. Occasional coaching when a student gets stuck—especially if they know what to ask for—is not a problem. However, if a parent finds their child needs to be taught the homework, that is a red flag. It is worth contacting the teacher and asking about it. Just doing the homework for the child, or even reteaching without finding out what the problem is, short-circuits the formative learning cycle and can even get in the way of learning.

FOR FURTHER READING

Cooper, H. (2001). Homework for all—in moderation. *Educational Leadership, 58*(7), 34–38. https://www.ascd.org/el/articles/homework-for-all-in-moderation

Ley, R., Knighton, B., Botwinski, B., Middlestead, S., & Alleman, J. (2010). Homework done right. *Educational Leadership, 68*(1). https://www.ascd.org/el/articles/homework-done-right

Marzano, R. J., & Pickering, D. J. (2007). The case for and against homework. *Educational Leadership, 64*(6), 74–79. https://www.ascd.org/el/articles/the-case-for-and-against-homework

Pope, D. (2020). *Quality over quantity: Elements of effective homework.* https://challengesuccess.org/wp-content/uploads/2021/04/Challenge-Success-Homework-White-Paper-2020.pdf

Vatterott, C. (2018). *Rethinking homework: Best practices that support diverse needs* (2nd ed.). ASCD.

8

Deciding on Instructional Follow-Up

What Is Instructional Follow-Up?

One of the main purposes of classroom formative assessment, whether pre-assessment or assessment during learning, is to help teachers decide on next instructional moves. Research has found that this is difficult for many teachers, who may be better at interpreting assessment information than deciding what to do about it. This chapter presents a method based on looking at student work to uncover student thinking rather than correctness and considering a range of options for instructional follow-up, from most to least formative, based on teachers' understanding of student thinking related to intended learning goals and criteria.

Why Is Instructional Follow-Up Important?

Ongoing instruction can proceed in several ways. One way is to follow textbooks or other materials more or less in order. This approach is a play-to-the-middle strategy, assuming most commercially or locally developed materials are based on students' typical development in an area or on some sort of task analysis (e.g., one-digit addition comes before two-digit addition). In the absence of other information, this might be a good idea for most of the students, most of the time.

However, other information *is* available. Information from assessing students' work in daily lessons, used formatively, can help teachers target instruction precisely. To do this, teachers need to examine student work for evidence of student thinking rather than correctness. Assessing correctness alone leads to decisions about next instructional moves like review and practice on learning goals where students score low, without attention to why that might be. Reteaching what didn't work before and expecting a different result is not the best use of teacher or student time. However, when teachers look at student work with an eye toward understanding student thinking, next instructional moves can target specific misunderstandings or misconceptions, a more efficient road to improvement than just general practice. Next instructional moves can also play to student strengths, interests, and cultural capital.

How Do I Use Instructional Follow-Up in My Teaching and Assessing?

The key to targeted instructional follow-up is looking at student work to understand student thinking. That happens best when student work is a response to a quality task that elicited student thinking. Begin with a learning target or goal. What are students trying to learn? Then, assess the work they are doing to learn it. This can be classwork or sometimes homework; the important thing is that the task and student work are carefully matched to the learning target so they serve as a clear indicator of student thinking. Where are the students now? How does their work, individually and collectively, show that they are thinking about it? Given that, are there things your next instruction should clarify? What are the immediate next steps in thinking that the students need to take to move closer to the learning target?

Giving effective feedback (see Chapter 4) on the work can be the start of a next instructional move, where the next lesson plan includes an activity where students get to reflect on the feedback and use it in some way, for example to revise an assignment or to change their study strategies.

Beyond that, Brookhart and Oakley (2021) have organized a menu of possible next instructional moves, from most to least formative (Figure 8.1). This chart is a generalized version of a chart based on the work of Ruiz-Primo and her colleagues, who studied actual next instructional moves in mathematics and science, which was presented in Ruiz-Primo and Brookhart (2018). Figure 8.1 describes the various follow-up instructional choices that teachers in many subject areas might make.

Design next instructional moves to be as formative as possible. As previous chapters have shown, formative work requires a classroom climate that

FIGURE 8.1
Possible Next Instructional Moves, from Least to Most Formative

Evaluative — No Student Participation	Descriptive — No Student Participation	Descriptive — Minimal Student Participation	Descriptive — Student Participation	Descriptive — Students Coconstruct Meaning
• Go over the assignment with students, providing correct answers. • Go on with instruction as planned even though some students are not ready.	• Describe the task again. Go on with instruction as planned after this brief reclarification.	• Show students how to do the work, either by modeling or by reviewing an example. • Show additional examples. • Repeat elements of the previous lesson in the same manner as taught the first time. • Assign additional reading or viewing.	• Have students help demonstrate how to solve the problem. • Facilitate a short class discussion about the concept, issue, or task. • Present a minilesson focused on specific areas of need. • Have students revise their work (if the task is open-ended) or do additional practice questions (if the questions are right/wrong) according to the feedback they received. • Reteach the lesson (or part of it) with different materials and activities than before. • Build background knowledge if needed. • Present opportunities for students to apply ideas with active learning methods (which differ by subject area).	• Deconstruct the task or assignment with students, helping them see how what they are learning in this task connects with prior learning and with intended future learning. • Have students revise their work (if the task is open-ended) or do additional practice questions (if the questions are right/wrong) according to the feedback they received and reflect on what they learned by doing that. • Differentiate the next lesson, taking into account the variety of student starting points. • Offer students opportunities to choose an alternate way to show their thinking (e.g., create a speech, research a topic of interest, do an inquiry project).

Least Formative ⟵   ⟶ Most Formative

Source: From *How to Look at Student Work to Uncover Student Thinking* (p. 76), by S. M. Brookhart & A. Oakley, 2021, ASCD. Copyright 2021 by ASCD.

values learning and does not penalize students for mistakes or misunderstandings. Making instructional decisions that push closer to the formative end of the continuum can help create that climate. In any case, do not interpret the least-to-most formative continuum as a bad-to-good continuum, but rather as a description of the range of instructional follow-up options you have, all of which you will probably use sometimes. In practice, aim to be as formative as possible. You will find that as you do, formative, student-centered teaching becomes more of a go-to strategy for you.

Notice that the least formative instructional follow-up simply informs students "how they did" on their work. More helpful for learning are descriptive uses of formative assessment information, and these are described along a range of amount of student participation, from none through minimal and more, through instructional follow-up that engages students in coconstructing meaning. The latter are the strategies highlighted in the next section.

How Do I Involve Students in Instructional Follow-Up?

When you use instructional follow-up activities where students coconstruct meaning, you maximize students' use of the formative learning cycle. As they are trying to learn something, first they need to know what it is (Where am I going?), and then they need to know where they are now and where they should go next. Deconstructing the task students have done, using participatory techniques like class discussion, partner reflection, or small-group processing, will help students with all three of these aspects of learning—even clarifying the learning target, which will get clearer as students work with it. Following up on teacher, peer, or self-assessment feedback by having students revise their work also helps students with all three aspects of learning. If the student work was a set of questions and after your feedback students already know the correct answers, instead of revising, have students do additional similar practice questions.

Often, instructional follow-up decisions after looking at student work involve various methods of differentiation. There's really no going back. Once you understand a student's thinking, it's impossible—or at least existentially difficult—to ignore that and just proceed as if you didn't. As a teacher involved in one of my first projects about formative assessment observed, "Once you have information about where each student is, you're sort of obligated to differentiate."

Differentiation methods are wide-ranging and generally adapt one or more of the following: content (sources and materials), processes (the exercises and activities students do to learn), and products (the tasks students complete to demonstrate learning).

Consider an example of a differentiation strategy that adjusts content. Students are learning that all living things have life cycles. A close look at student work comparing the life cycle of a butterfly to the life cycle of humans suggests that some students have simply copied materials about butterflies but do not yet understand the cyclic development of living things. In a follow-up lesson, students are given questions to scaffold that thinking and are routed to different print and internet resources for information. Some students use simple diagrams, others use text and pictures from a science textbook, and some use more complex text, pictures, or videos from more advanced sources.

For the same lesson, consider a differentiation strategy that adjusts the process. Students are given the same set of scaffolded questions designed to move thinking from categorizing life stages to developing the idea of cyclic development. The teacher constructs heterogeneous groups, based on the formative assessment, and asks students to work together to write group answers to a set of questions, which they will post on a bulletin board app.

Yet another differentiation strategy might be to adjust the product. Different students are given different versions of the scaffolded questions, based on their current level of understanding. Some ask basic questions that lead students to the idea of lifetime development. Others who are ready get questions that ask them to extend their understanding of life cycles by applying the ideas to other living things.

The key point for all of these is that the selection of strategy should be based on formative assessment information, and the strategy should help each student make an immediate next step toward the learning target or goal. Further, that formative assessment information should come from looking at student work for evidence of student thinking more than correctness. The Further Reading list includes some resources for additional differentiation strategies.

What Are Some Common Misconceptions About Instructional Follow-Up?

One misconception about instructional follow-up is that it will take up time and ruin instructional pacing. This is only true if you consider "pacing" as the teacher covering some material. If you think of pacing as students learning the material, you will find that targeted instructional follow-up actually speeds up the process. It short-circuits the trial-and-error aspects of some lessons: just teach a little bit of all of it and they'll get something out of it. In addition, the follow-up described in this chapter does not have to be time-consuming or elaborate. The purpose of the chart in Figure 8.1 was to help simplify instructional decisions so that effective and efficient follow-up can become routine.

Another misconception about targeted instructional follow-up is that it will always come as a surprise and wreak havoc on long-term planning. In fact, sometimes when you look at student work with an eye toward uncovering student thinking, what you learn is that most students are in fact on track and therefore your next lesson is on track, as well.

Some teachers think that instructional follow-up based on formative assessment information means individualizing learning. This is not true. Although some teachers may individualize instruction for selected students, differentiation does not mean individualization. No teacher could make separate lesson plans for each student—nor is that necessary.

Finally, some teachers think that instructional follow-up that differentiates learning will mean some students do not achieve the standards. The goal of looking at student work for evidence of student thinking and then using appropriate instructional follow-up is that more, not fewer, students achieve intended learning goals.

FOR FURTHER READING

Andrade, H. L., & Heritage, M. (2018). *Using formative assessment to enhance learning, achievement, and academic self-regulation.* Routledge.

Brookhart, S. M., & Oakley, A. (2021). *How to look at student work to uncover student thinking.* ASCD.

Ruiz-Primo, M. A., & Brookhart, S. M. (2018). *Using feedback to improve learning.* Routledge.

Tomlinson, C. A. (2017). *How to differentiate instruction in academically diverse classrooms* (3rd ed.). ASCD.

9

Using Curriculum-Based Measurement

What Is Curriculum-Based Measurement?

Curriculum-based *assessment* (CBA) is a practice that involves direct observation and scoring of students' performance on critical skills in a subject or grade level. CBA has three defining qualities (Fuchs & Fuchs, 2007a, 2007b): assessment materials are aligned with the school's curriculum; measurement happens frequently; and results are used for instructional decision making. Proponents argue that, given the choice between CBA and commercial standardized test results for instructional decision making, curriculum-based measures are more appropriate and effective because the tasks in those assessments link directly to what students are expected to learn and what they are taught.

One form of CBA is curriculum-based *measurement* (CBM), which emphasizes standardized tasks that are brief and easy to administer, resulting in alternate forms of roughly equivalent difficulty suitable for making comparisons across time, and quantitative analysis of progress using graphs. Elements that are standardized in CBM include the tasks and directions for administering them, the time limit for students to do each task, and the scoring rules teachers use to score student responses. Curriculum-based measurement was developed as a means for elementary school teachers of students with disabilities to track key outcomes in reading and mathematics. Since then, it has been applied more broadly, for example, for progress monitoring to support response to intervention.

CBM differs from other classroom formative assessment in that the measures are repeated measures of a general outcome (e.g., words per minute read) rather than measures of smaller-grained learning goals. Also in contrast to other classroom formative assessment, CBM is typically more teacher-centered than student-centered.

Why Is Curriculum-Based Measurement Important?

Curriculum-based measurement is particularly important for monitoring student progress in early literacy and numeracy. In these areas, sets of parallel measures can be easily constructed and scored and the results compared. In addition, such skills are foundational and fundamental for literacy and numeracy education. Experiments with curriculum-based measurement beyond early literacy and numeracy have met with some success in writing, math computation, math problem solving, and even algebra.

Some authors consider any curriculum-based sequence of tests a kind of curriculum-based assessment (Blankenship, 1985). For example, a teacher might give a pre-test, mid-test, and post-test in a unit of instruction to track progress on specific instructional objectives, for the purpose of identifying students' needs for remediation or moving on. In contrast, this chapter will focus on describing the use of CBM for early literacy and numeracy, where the learning domains are relatively finite and lend themselves well to repeated measures. For more complex learning objectives, and especially for learning objectives where taking a pre-test would cause many students to begin a unit with a failure experience, I recommend a broader approach to pre-assessment (see Chapter 3) and a more student-centered approach to formative assessment (see Chapters 1 through 7) as the most effective assessments to support teaching and learning.

How Do I Use Curriculum-Based Measurement in My Teaching and Assessment?

Teachers in any class can use CBM to monitor the progress of all students or selected students, for use in their own instructional decision making. CBM is also used as a progress monitoring tool in the Response to Intervention (RTI) process of identifying students with special needs. CBM uses a series of brief samples of student performance, called probes, each taking one to five minutes. Typically, probes are administered once or twice a week for progress monitoring and instructional decision making, although monthly or other schedules have been used.

Several very thorough manuals for educators are available that detail the steps needed to create, administer, score, analyze, and evaluate CBM probes (Fuchs & Fuchs, 2007a, 2007b; Wright, n.d.). You should consult those manuals if you need directions that are detailed enough to set up your own CBM program. This chapter provides an orientation to how CBM is conducted. My intention is to give readers enough information to understand what CBM attempts to do, what the results look like, and how they inform instructional decisions.

Basic Steps for CBM

The basic CBM process is very similar to other assessment processes: set the purpose, create the CBM probes, administer and score the CBM probes, analyze the data (typically by creating a CBM chart), and evaluate the results and their implications for instruction.

Set purpose. As with all assessment, the first step in conducting CBM is deciding what it is you want to measure and monitor. For early literacy and numeracy, common domains of interest include, for example, the following: letter naming fluency, letter sound fluency, phoneme segmentation fluency, word identification fluency, and oral reading fluency in reading; and number identification, missing number, and quantity discrimination in mathematics. Other learning domains of interest can be identified (e.g., addition facts to 20, all spelling words in a grade-level spelling book). The key is that the learning domain of interest is a basic skill that spans the curricular year, so that you can track progress, as opposed to, for example, using as the domain just those spelling words you were going to teach this week. Because you are going to invest in tracking this skill over time, you would want to select a very important skill, either because of its place in your curriculum or because of its relevance to a particular student's needs, or both. Once you have identified the domain of interest, the set of materials from which you will construct your probes is easy to identify. For example, if you are using CBM to monitor addition facts to 20, there is a finite number of facts from 0 + 0 to 10 + 10.

Create CBM probes. To create CBM probes, you randomly sample from the set of materials that represent your learning domain of interest. Students take a different form of the probe each time, but they are randomly equivalent. After selecting the tasks (the items or questions) for each probe, construct student and teacher copies. The teacher's version is also a score sheet that you can mark with your observations and on which you can calculate the student's score.

For common domains of interest, especially in early literacy and numeracy, you can find digital resources that do the sampling and probe construction for you. Some of these are free and available on the internet, and others are products for sale by vendors.

Administer and score CBM probes. Administration and scoring of CBM probes differs by subject. Specific scoring rules for reading, writing, spelling, and mathematics probes can be found in the above-referenced manuals. Scoring rules for CBM probes are point systems, where certain qualities of the performance (e.g., a correct digit or a correct word) are given points, which are then added up. CBM probes are not scored right/wrong as is common for a typical classroom test question or with rubrics as is common for typical classroom performance assessments. Strict adherence to the scoring rules is part of what makes the CBM scores comparable over time and underscores the validity of the graphing and tracking analyses used for CBM.

Set up CBM chart. CBM scores are typically tracked in a CBM chart. Figure 9.1 is a simple example. Some CBM charts also have vertical lines that separate baseline scores (if there are more than one) from monitoring scores and then mark changes in instruction if any are made. For oral reading fluency and other CBM probes that you expect to be variable, baseline is typically considered the median of three probes. For letter naming and other simpler learning domains, one probe can be used to establish a baseline.

To keep the graph simple, Figure 9.1 assumes that a baseline of 30 words read correctly per minute (wcpm) has been established for our fictional student. A more complex graph would have graphed the three baseline probes, the median of which would be 30 wcpm, and then dropped a vertical line after the first three observations to indicate that monitoring has begun.

The next step is to set the goal. This can be done using grade-level norms for reading or other skills, or by calculating expected progress for a particular student. In Figure 9.1, the teacher expected that the student would read approximately 2 additional wcpm per week, for 10 weeks, arriving at a goal of 50 wcpm after 10 weeks. Another student's goal might be more ambitious, for example 3 additional wcpm per week to arrive at 60 wcpm at week 10.

Once you have the baseline and a goal, connect the two with a straight line. This line is often called a goal line or aimline. It can be adjusted; as you monitor the student's progress you also monitor the appropriateness of the goal. During monitoring, students' actual probe scores are graphed and the dots are connected as in Figure 9.1. CBM management software is available for school districts to purchase, or you can use a spreadsheet.

FIGURE 9.1
Example Curriculum-Based Measurement Chart for One Student

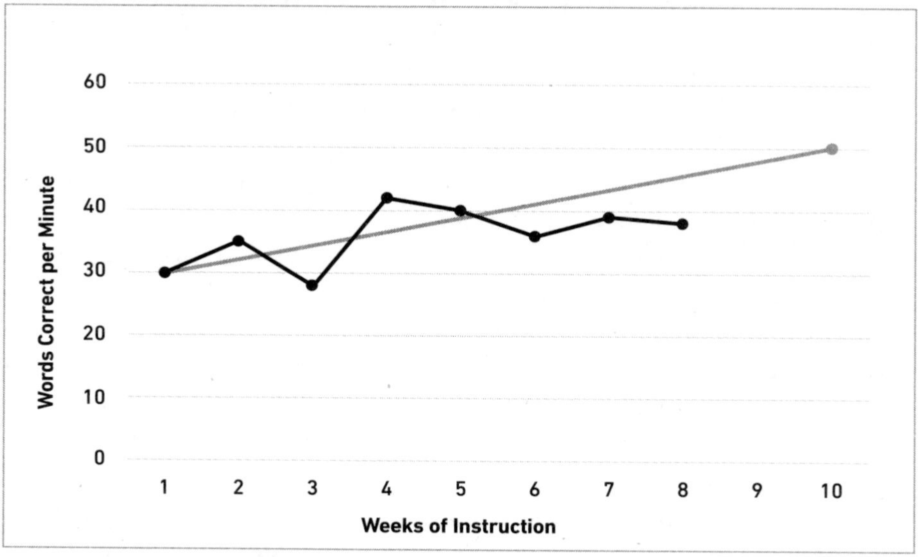

Note: The straight line is the aimline. The jagged line is student performance.

Evaluate CBM results. Evaluating CBM results is an ongoing process of comparing student's actual performance with the goal line. The simplest evaluation of CBM results involves visual inspection of the graph. If the student scores above the goal line three times in a row, you adjust (increase) the goal. If the student scores below the goal line three times in a row, you adjust instruction. When that happens, you can mark the graph with a vertical line so you can note the rate of progress before and after the change in instruction. If a student scores around the goal line three times in a row (on it, or two above/one below or vice versa), you consider that instruction is appropriate for meeting the goal and make no changes. You can see that the student in Figure 9.1 has scored below the goal line three times in a row, at weeks 6, 7, and 8. The teacher would then decide that instruction needs to be changed in some way, often by changing the duration, frequency, or group size for the instruction. She would drop a vertical line at week 8, to indicate that instruction changed, and then continue to monitor the student's progress.

Other Uses of CBM

Additional statistical analysis is possible with data from students' CBM probes. Once you have seven or eight data points, you can calculate a trendline to measure the student's rate of growth in performance. The most common way to do this is called the Tukey Method. If you need to calculate the trendline by hand, the Tukey Method is detailed in the manuals. Commonly, however, you can use CBM software to do it. Then instead of the simple "three data points" decision rules, you can compare the slopes of the trendline and the goal line. If the trendline is steeper than the goal line, you can adjust the student's end-of-year goal; if the trendline is flatter than the goal line, you can revise the student's instructional program. Of course, if the trendline and goal line match, you don't need to make any changes in either the goal or the instruction.

Another analysis that can be helpful is the calculation of local norms for CBM probes. Calculating local (classroom or school) norms allows you to compare students' performance with that of their peers. For common CBM probes in early literacy and numeracy, you can also find national norms for rates of growth and end-of-year benchmarks.

CBM can also be used for accountability, in several ways. The number of students in a school who meet CBM benchmarks can be reported, and schools can set goals to increase those numbers within a school year or over successive years. CBM can also be used to monitor teachers' progress, by plotting the number of students on track to meet CBM benchmarks over a school year. Finally, CBM can be used to monitor a school's special education performance, again by plotting the number of students on track to meet CBM benchmarks over the school year.

How Do I Involve Students in Curriculum-Based Measurement?

Curriculum-based measurement is typically used to change teacher instruction and then indirectly to improve student learning. It is not typically thought of as a vehicle for student involvement. However, I have seen resourceful teachers share CBM goals with their students, using goal sheets, and have students join in tracking and celebrating progress.

What Are Some Common Misconceptions About Curriculum-Based Measurement?

Some educators think of curriculum-based assessment and curriculum-based measurement as the same thing. As this chapter has shown, CBM is a very specific, well-developed, and well-researched form of CBA that can, when used well, help students who struggle receive the instruction they need. There has been much less research and development on CBA in general. Of course, almost all classroom assessment is keyed to the curriculum in some way, and effective teachers use classroom assessment to gather the information they need to make the decisions they need to make, whether or not they use a systematic repeated-measures format.

FOR FURTHER READING

Blankenship, C. S. (1985). Using curriculum-based assessment data to make instructional decisions. *Exceptional Children, 52*(3), 233–238.

Clarke, S. (2009). Using curriculum-based measurement to improve achievement. *Principal,* 30–33.

Fuchs, L. S., & Fuchs, D. (2007a). *Using CBM for progress monitoring in reading.* U.S. Office of Special Education Programs: Ideas that Work. https://files.eric.ed.gov/fulltext/ED519252.pdf

Fuchs, L. S., & Fuchs, D. (2007b). *Using CBM for progress monitoring in written expression and spelling.* U.S. Office of Special Education Programs: Ideas that Work. https://files.eric.ed.gov/fulltext/ED519251.pdf

Intervention Central. (2022). Response to intervention resources. https://www.interventioncentral.org/

Lembke, E. S., & Stecker, P. M. (2007). *Curriculum-based measurement in mathematics: An evidence-based formative assessment procedure.* RMC Research Corporation, Center on Instruction. https://files.eric.ed.gov/fulltext/ED521574.pdf

Wright, J. (n.d.) *Curriculum-based measurement: A manual for teachers.* http://www.jimwrightonline.com/pdfdocs/cbaManual.pdf

10

Making Accommodations in Assessment

What Are Accommodations in Assessment?

Accommodations in assessment are changes made to the conditions or materials of an assessment that do not alter the construct (the learning goal) being measured. Accommodations can be specified in students' individualized education programs (IEP). Accommodations are often contrasted with modifications, which are changes in the conditions or materials of assessment that do alter the construct being measured. The purpose of accommodations is to give students with disabilities or special needs access to assessment.

Why Are Accommodations Important?

Assessment is an important part of teaching and learning. Students can only participate in the formative learning cycle if they receive feedback and other forms of assessment information. Teachers can only target instruction if they have sound assessment information. Some assessment methods and formats present barriers to certain students that are not part of the construct being measured. For example, students with reading difficulties may not do well on a mathematics test not because they didn't understand the problems, but because they had difficulty reading them. If the problems are read to the student, they can show what they know about the mathematics.

The same would not be the case for a reading test, where being able to read the material is part of what is being assessed.

A common exercise used in professional development is to find a willing participant who wears eyeglasses and ask her to look at a test without her glasses. "Wait!" she might say. "I can't read the test without my glasses. How am I supposed to answer the questions?" This is the principle for accommodations. With glasses—with accommodations, whatever they are in a particular student's case—the student can complete the assessment and benefit from its results. The results are comparable to any other student completing the same assessment.

How Do I Use Accommodations in My Assessment?

Accommodations in assessment and instruction go hand in hand. Typically, students have similar accommodations in both. For example, a student who needs large print instructional materials would need large print assessment materials. A student who needs extra time for instructional activities may need extra time for assessment. Coordinate assessment and instruction so that students get the accommodations they need—and are used to—for both.

This chapter takes the stance that the best approach to accommodations in assessment is to design assessments using principles of universal design for learning (UDL) in the first place, offering the widest possible accessibility without making individual accommodations, and then making individual accommodations as necessary (Jung, 2023). Given this assumption, follow these general steps to select and use accommodations in assessment:

1. Identify the learning goal or target to be taught and assessed and share it with students.
2. Prepare materials for instruction and assessment according to UDL principles.
3. Identify individual students who still need assistance accessing the materials.
4. Using professional judgment, activate appropriate affordances available to any student who needs them, described below as universal features or designated features.
5. Identify individual students who still need assistance accessing the materials.
6. Using an IEP or 504 plan, activate accommodations appropriate to the individual student's needs.

As mentioned, accommodations for instruction and assessment should for the most part be similar. For example, if a student may use a bilingual dictionary during instruction, they may use it during assessment. Never use an accommodation for the first time during an assessment. If special circumstances dictate that an accommodation will not be used during an assessment—whether a classroom assessment or a standardized assessment—give the student opportunity to practice the skill to be assessed without the accommodation.

Finally, be aware that in accommodation, more is not always better. The key is to match the accommodation with the student's specific need and with the specific learning goal being measured. A dictionary that helps one student may be a distraction to another. Reading questions aloud may be useful in mathematics but interfere with assessment of the learning goal in reading. Students themselves are a good source of information about what accommodations help them (see the section on Involving Students in Accommodations below).

Universal Design for Learning

Think of UDL as removing barriers for all learners, no matter their special need, language, or other status. The three UDL guidelines are (CAST, 2018):

- Provide multiple means of engagement.
- Provide multiple means of representation.
- Provide multiple means of action and expression.

Multiple means of engagement spark different students' interest, effort, self-regulation, and background experiences, in school and out. For example, give students choices about their work. Help students focus and avoid distractions by removing irrelevant material, clarifying learning goals, giving goal-oriented feedback, and helping students develop habits of self-regulation.

Multiple means of representation of content stimulate different students' perceptions and appropriation of material. Offer alternative presentations of auditory, visual, and textual information in various media. Clarify key terms and vocabulary. Make sure students understand the format of material. Activate prior knowledge—and where needed, supply background knowledge—and help students understand the big ideas or essential questions underlying the content. Provide opportunities for transfer and generalization of knowledge, so it does not remain locked in one context.

Multiple means of action and expression activate different students' response options. Consider various physical, verbal, graphic, or other response options in various media. Help students set goals and plan and manage their learning. In other words, help students participate in the formative learning cycle. An illustration comes to mind. Remember the first phones that allowed texting? At first, sending a text meant repeatedly poking the numeric keypad to get to each letter. Smartphones allowed keyboard use—still poking with a thumb or finger but much quicker. Then came Swype keyboards that allowed for more efficient finger action. Some newer smartphones have a microphone icon that allows audio texts, no typing required. All of us, not just those who are keyboard-challenged, benefit from these increasingly helpful means of expression.

Instruction and assessment that use these guidelines remove barriers to instruction and assessment for many students by giving them different pathways into the content and different pathways to respond to it. Analogous to the way curb cuts benefit not only wheelchairs but also strollers, people carrying heavy boxes, people with sore feet, and a host of other things, UDL guidelines benefit all students, not just those with special needs. Use UDL principles for all of your instruction and assessment methods and materials. This is actually a timesaver, because it will reduce the amount of accommodation you need to do. When UDL principles are observed, more students will be able to participate without accommodations.

Universal Features and Designated Features

Shyyan and colleagues (2016) distinguish three tiers of accessibility supports for students in instruction, classroom assessment, and state accountability assessment: universal features, designated features, and accommodations. *Universal features* can be made generally available for any student who needs or wants them, regardless of disability status. For example, some teachers allow students to use dictionaries or calculators, take breaks, use highlighters or spellcheck, use scratch paper, and so on, depending on the learning goal and the instructional activity or assessment. Digital materials allow students to change the size of text fonts or graphics and sometimes the color or other features.

Designated features are accessibility supports that any student may have if a qualified educator or educator team has determined a need. Examples include using a bilingual dictionary, having a human reader or using a text-to-speech application, and native language translation of general test directions. There are also some administrative considerations available to any student who needs them, for example, adaptive furniture, the opportunity to take an assessment in a quiet place free of distractions, or even receiving encouragement.

Accommodations

Accommodations, as defined earlier, are accessibility supports for students with special needs and are documented in Individualized Education Programs or 504 plans. The Council of Chief State School Officers (Thompson et al., 2005) described accommodations for state tests in five categories: presentation accommodations, equipment/material accommodations, response accommodations, scheduling/timing accommodations, and setting accommodations. In a more recent publication, the Council of Chief State School Officers (Shyyan et al., 2016) has used the term "accessibility supports," reserving the term "accommodations" for those that must be prescribed in an IEP or 504 plan. In addition to accommodations, accessibility supports include the universal and designated features described above, which also typically belong to one of the five categories.

Jung and her colleagues (2019) have organized these types of accommodations in a manner helpful for classroom instruction and assessment. They describe accommodations in size, time, input, output, and level of support (Figure 10.1).

FIGURE 10.1
Types of Accommodations

Type	Definition	Examples
Size	Reduces the number of items a student must complete, with no change to difficulty	• The student is assigned 10 multiplication problems rather than 20, but the difficulty of problems is not altered.
Time	Adjusts amount of time allotted for learning, task completion, or testing	• The student is allowed extra time to complete a test.
Input	Specifies the way instruction is delivered to the learner	• The student gets guided notes for use in Earth Science.
Output	Specifies how the learner can respond to instruction	• The student creates a poster instead of writing a research paper for World History. • The student dictates answers to worksheet questions about addition facts.
Level of support	Identifies the amount of personal assistance to an individual learner	• The student uses a Livescribe pen to record a conversation with a teacher for later use in writing. • A peer helps the student with the physical construction of a diorama of the first mission in California.

Source: From *Your Students, My Students, Our Students: Rethinking Equitable and Inclusive Classrooms* (p. 24) by L. A. Jung, N. Frey, D. Fisher, & J. Kroener, 2019, ASCD. Copyright 2019 by ASCD.

Key in selecting accommodations for students is a match to student needs in the context of the learning goal that is assessed. For example, students who have short attention spans may benefit from accommodations in the size of an assignment. Students with physical disabilities (e.g., poor vision) may benefit from accommodations of time. Students with reading disabilities may benefit from accommodations in input. Students with writing disabilities may benefit from accommodations of output. The level of support can be adjusted to individual students' needs. Please understand that these are just examples, not prescriptions for assigning accommodations and certainly not a complete list of disabilities or available accommodations. The point here is that the specific accommodation chosen must match a student's need, and must, in fact, help address the need. As you use accommodations, evaluate their suitability and their effectiveness by observing the student and the work and by consulting with the student.

How Do I Involve Students in Accommodations?

Students are an excellent source of information on how an accommodation is working. For students who are able, reflection forms or journals can be helpful. Or you can talk with the student. They can offer information about what accommodations they used during instruction and assessment—students do not always use all accommodations that are offered. They can reflect on the results of their classroom assignments and assessment and offer an opinion on how well the accommodation worked. They can give their perspectives on difficulties or barriers they may have encountered when trying to use an accommodation.

Information from student reflection forms or journals, or information from teacher notes documenting conversations with students, can be used to adjust ongoing classroom instruction and assessment. This information can also inform the development of students' IEPs.

What Are Some Common Misconceptions About Accommodations?

One common misconception is that accommodations are not fair to other students. For example, if one student gets extra time to do something, why doesn't everyone get extra time? This misconception is basically a confusion between equality (everyone getting the same thing) and equity (everyone getting what they need). Teachers can help students understand that not everyone needs the same thing. Not everyone needs glasses, for example.

They can also point out that in class, when they use their time wisely, everyone really does get the time they need to do assignments and other tasks.

Another misconception is one that this chapter may have helped to dispel. Some may think that accommodations make assessments "easier" for some students than others. This is not—or should not be—true. Some *modifications* do this, as for example, when an assessment is based on a simplified learning standard. But an appropriate accommodation simply removes irrelevant barriers to students' demonstration of what they know on the same learning goals as other students.

FOR FURTHER READING

CAST. (2018). *Universal Design for Learning Guidelines version 2.2.* http://udlguidelines.cast.org

Jung, L. A. (2023). *Seen, heard, and valued: Universal design for learning and beyond.* Corwin.

Jung, L. A., Frey, N., Fisher, D., & Kroener, J. (2019). *Your students, my students, our students: Rethinking equitable and inclusive classrooms.* ASCD.

Shyyan, V., Thurlow, M., Christensen, L., Lazarus, S., Paul, J., & Touchette, B. (2016). *CCSSO accessibility manual: How to select, administer, and evaluate use of accessibility supports for instruction and assessment of all students.* CCSSO. https://learning.ccsso.org/council-of-chief-state-school-officers-ccsso-accessibility-manual-how-to-select-administer-and-evaluate-use-of-accessibility-supports-for-instruction-and-assessment-of-all-students

Thompson, S. J., Morse, A. B., Sharpe, M., & Hall, S. (2005). *CCSSO accommodations manual: How to select, administer, and evaluate use of accommodations for instruction and assessment of students with disabilities.* CCSSO.

11

Supporting Equity and Fairness in Assessment

What Are Equity and Fairness in Assessment?

Equity in assessment is typically conceived as using assessment to meet students' varying needs, which entails treating different students differently. In this way it differs from *equality* or treating all students the same. *Fairness* in assessment typically also involves the perceptions and reactions of the students who are assessed. Because classrooms are socially constructed environments, the beliefs and perceptions of the teachers and students help shape what is considered fair in assessment and in other aspects of classroom life. Because of differences in backgrounds, experiences, and developmental levels, both teachers and students hold a range of ideas about what is fair. Fairness is also one of the goals of culturally relevant and culturally sustaining assessment (Ladson-Billings, 2014).

Fairness in standardized testing can be defined as "the validity of test score interpretation for intended use(s) for individuals from all relevant subgroups" (American Educational Research Association et al., 2014, p. 219). A chapter in *Standards for Educational and Psychological Testing* explores general views of fairness in measurement, threats to fair and valid interpretations of test scores, and ways to minimize construct-irrelevant variance in test scores. As you can see, this view emphasizes whether the score is a fair measure of what it's supposed to measure. In other words, a student is treated fairly if that student is well measured. Recently, Randall (2021) and others have argued that this traditional view of the construct to be measured, as if it existed in a color-neutral universe, provides an "illusion of fairness" (p. 85) but actually centers assessment on the understandings of the dominant (white) culture. In other words, she takes issue with current ways in which what a test is supposed to measure is defined. This debate is likely to continue, and ideas about fairness in standardized testing are changing.

In classroom assessment, the idea of fairness includes an additional layer of complexity even beyond debates about defining and measuring constructs fairly. Classroom assessment is situated in a sociocultural environment where teaching, learning, and assessment take place. Therefore, fairness in classroom assessment also includes the perceptions of students, teachers, and parents. Students are not just examinees to be measured but also active learners. Their perceptions affect both their performance on assessments and how they respond to the results. Studies of fairness in classroom assessment have identified six important issues (Rasooli et al., 2018): (1) opportunity to learn; (2) transparency, consistency, and justification of the criteria used for feedback and grading; (3) appropriate use of accommodations; (4) a constructive classroom environment and the "do no harm" principle; (5) avoiding bias and distortion in assessment results; and (6) considerations related to group work and peer assessment.

Why Are Equity and Fairness in Assessment Important?

Many people value equity and fairness as social values in their own right. Beyond that "general good" argument, perceptions and beliefs are an important determining factor in student and teacher behavior, and that includes teaching and learning behaviors in the classroom. Further, when equity and fairness goals are pursued in assessment, students are better able to show what they know. Higher-quality assessment evidence leads to better feedback, more targeted instruction, improved learning, and more valid grades.

How Do I Use Equitable and Fair Practices in My Teaching and Assessment?

Figure 11.1 summarizes some practices that support equitable and fair assessment. This list is a compilation from various sources, but it is not exhaustive. These practices are recommended for all students, including students with disabilities and English learners. Check the "For Further

FIGURE 11.1
Strategies to Support Equity and Fairness in Classroom Assessment

- Identify, state clearly, and share learning goals in appropriate student-facing and culturally relevant language. Share criteria for success and check for student understanding.
- Involve students in assessment. Leverage students' interests, experiences, and cultural funds of knowledge in assessment and instruction.
- Use appropriate accommodations in assessment and instruction. Provide scaffolding as needed, including language scaffolding for English learners.
- Differentiate assessment and instruction when needed.
- Check for sources of bias in assessment materials and procedures.
- Use ungraded formative assessment and ensure appropriate opportunity to learn before administering summative (graded) assessment.
- Use multiple sources of evidence of learning.
- Allow students to redo and revise as appropriate to demonstrate learning.

Reading" section for additional ideas. All students deserve to feel that their assessment is equitable and fair.

Social psychology suggests fairness has three dimensions to attend to in classroom assessment. Distributive justice means students perceive that the distribution of outcomes, like grades or opportunities, is fair. Procedural justice means students perceive that the procedures used for outcome distribution, like grading practices, are fair. Interactional justice means students perceive interpersonal relationships are fair, for example, treating all students with respect or communicating clearly to everyone. The strategies in Figure 11.1 are practical ways that teachers can enact those three dimensions in their classroom assessment.

Identify, State Clearly, and Share Learning Goals in Appropriate Student-Facing and Culturally Relevant Language

Sharing learning goals and criteria for success, and checking for student understanding of both, is the most fundamental thing you can do to create an atmosphere of equity and fairness in classroom assessment—and instruction, too. Teachers who work with learning targets and success criteria often come to realize they are an agent for equity because all students have access to the qualities of good work and tools to get them there. This can only happen if the targets are presented to students in ways they can understand and appropriate. Students who are aware of their targets and success criteria can actively aim for them, ask for help when needed, and monitor their own progress.

Involve Students in Assessment and Leverage Students' Interests, Experiences, and Cultural Funds of Knowledge in Assessment and Instruction

Involving students in assessment is almost always a good thing, not least because when students are part of the assessment process, they are more likely to perceive it as fair, and they can raise questions or issues as they arise. Using students' interests and experiences in assessment tasks and instructional activities also helps students perceive that they are known and heard.

There are many ways to involve students in assessment that will leverage their interests, experiences, and cultural funds of knowledge. You can, for example, give students some choice over when and how they show what they have learned. You can design performance assessments and scenario-based test questions that draw upon settings and situations that are familiar to the students, in language they would understand. You can provide assessment tasks that allow students multiple ways to solve problems, explain reasoning, or construct products. Students can be part of assessment by cocreating criteria, participating in self- and peer assessment, and participating in the interpretation and use of assessment results for formative purposes.

Use Appropriate Accommodations in Assessment and Instruction

Sound use of accommodations (see Chapter 10) contributes to fairness and equity in classroom assessment. Provide scaffolding as needed, including language scaffolding for English learners. Scaffolding comes in many forms. For example, you might break up an assessment into smaller chunks. You might provide a set of questions, sometimes called a self-assessment script, for students to consider when they are doing their work. You might provide help with directions for English learners or students who struggle with organization. Whatever the accommodation, the key is that it is matched to the student's specific needs, which is what makes it fair for all students.

Differentiate Assessment and Instruction When Needed

One of the things you can teach your students is that differentiated classrooms are much fairer than classrooms in which every student, no matter their background or experience with the material, are made to do the same assignments in the same way. Differentiation is a broader term than accommodation. Differentiation means deploying a variety of strategies and materials to help all students get the most out of their lessons. Differentiation involves providing accommodations in assessment and instruction to students who need them, true, but it also involves using a variety of instructional strategies, grouping strategies, feedback strategies, and so on. As differentiation expert Rick Wormeli writes (2018, p. 3): "If your teachers ever rephrased a question; extended a deadline; provided a few extra examples to help you understand something; stood next to you to keep your attention focused on the lesson; regrouped the class according to student interest, readiness, or the way students learned best; gave you a choice among assignments based on something they knew about you; or let you redo a test or project if at first you didn't succeed, they differentiated instruction."

One aspect of differentiation can be tiering assessments, which is the concept most likely to be confused with accommodation. Tiering means altering the complexity level of assignments or assessments to adjust the level of challenge for different students so that, for example, you might have two, or sometimes even three, versions of the same assignment or assessment. In a differentiated classroom, not every assignment or assessment is tiered. Using tiered assessments when warranted contributes to classroom fairness. Nevertheless, tiering is not accommodation. For example, if a student needs an English dictionary, or a braille version of an assessment, or any other accommodation described in Chapter 10, they should get that accommodation for every assessment, whether it is tiered or not. Differentiated instruction is a topic worthy of a whole book in itself. Interested readers should check the Further Reading list.

Check for Sources of Bias in Assessment Materials and Procedures

When assessment materials are of poor quality, the results can be biased. Thus, the first check for sources of bias is to ensure that your assessment materials—questions, tasks, rubrics, and so on—are a clear match with the learning you intend to measure and have been constructed according to the principles for quality in all the chapters in this book. In addition, check for sources of bias in assessment materials because of cultural insensitivity or irrelevance in the language, tasks, or procedures used. Finally, check student readiness for any assessment that you give. Student anxiety, lack of motivation, or lack of confidence can be a source of bias in assessment results, as well.

Use Ungraded Formative Assessment and Ensure Appropriate Opportunity to Learn Before Administering Summative (Graded) Assessment

Formative classroom assessment gives students information they can use to further their learning and gives the teacher evidence of when the student is ready for summative (graded) assessment. Formative classroom assessment is not graded so that no punishment is attached to the learning process; rather, formative classroom assessment receives actionable feedback for furthering learning. Formative classroom assessment is practice, which students do until they have achieved or at least approached the learning target and are ready to show what they know.

Use Multiple, Diverse Sources of Evidence of Learning

Using multiple sources of evidence helps with reliability and validity of assessment information. Anyone can do anything once, but when multiple sources of evidence converge on a result, teachers and students can have confidence in that result. Using multiple sources of evidence also helps with equity and fairness, because different sources of evidence engage different students' preferences and strengths. For example, the learning goals for a unit of instruction may be assessed with a unit test, an individual project, and a group task with individual output on a bulletin board app. These assessments may be weighted equally or differently in the grade, depending on their content and the learning outcomes assessed. The collection of three results gives a more well-rounded picture of student achievement than any one of them alone could.

Allow Students to Redo and Revise as Appropriate to Demonstrate Learning

Students learn at different rates, and therefore they become ready for summative (graded) assessment at different times. Teachers typically have way too many students to make it possible to give students individually timed assessments. Redo's and revisions are a next-best-thing strategy. Students who were not fully ready to show what they know on an assessment of a particular learning outcome may redo or revise the work, depending on what it is. For tests of facts and concepts, where the results of the assessment show students which questions they got wrong, use redo's. For example, give the student a set of math problems like the one on the test they are redoing, but not exactly the same problems. For performance assessments of how students apply, analyze, and use knowledge, use revisions. For example, a student may revise a written paper or a science project according to feedback. Typically, teachers ask students to apply for a redo or revision by specifying what they did to improve their understanding after the first assessment. This gives the teacher and student an opportunity to check that additional learning has in fact occurred. Treating students in this way is a respectful and fair way to handle students' differences in learning speeds and readiness.

How Do I Involve Students in Equity and Fairness in Assessment?

One simple way to involve students in equity and fairness in assessment is to teach these principles explicitly. Younger children especially sometimes think in terms of equality rather than equity (everyone gets one cookie). Students may perceive some assessment strategies done in the name of equity or fairness (e.g., shortened assignments for some students) as unfair. In fact, many teachers also think in those terms. Teaching students social justice principles fits with current ideas about teaching the whole child and social-emotional learning. Classroom discussions, demonstrations, and role plays about fairness in assessment can help students feel heard and taken seriously. Tackling these issues explicitly in the classroom can also help build a classroom climate that values equity and fairness, in assessment and in other matters.

What Are Some Common Misconceptions About Equity and Fairness in Assessment?

Probably the most common misconceptions about equity and fairness occur in the area of grading. Many teachers still argue that if they differentiate assessment, they are not being fair to other students. This may stem from a misconception about grading itself: grading is not a standardized test. Grading is a method of reporting students' current status on intended learning outcomes, for the information of students, parents and guardians, and others. Assessment that accomplishes that purpose is equitable, whether the methods are the same for all students or not. This contrasts with standardized tests, where standardized administration procedures are built into the process.

Not exactly a misconception, but still an important point to make, is that students in a class may have differing ideas on what is fair. It is not the case that if teachers just adhere to the principles in this chapter, or any other principles for equity and fairness, then all students will be happy. In general, though, the more students perceive their classroom learning environment, including the classroom assessment environment, to be fair, the more comfortable students will be with learning and assessment.

FOR FURTHER READING

American Educational Research Association, American Psychological Association, & National Council on Measurement in Education. (2014). *Standards for educational and psychological testing.* American Educational Research Association.

Datnow, A., & Park, V. (2019). *Using data for equity in the classroom* (quick reference guide). ASCD.

Feldman, J. (2019). *Grading for equity: What it is, why it matters, and how it can transform schools and classrooms.* Corwin.

Ladson-Billings, G. (2014). Culturally relevant pedagogy 2.0: a.k.a. the remix. *Harvard Educational Review, 84*(1), 74–84.

Randall, J. (2021). "Color-neutral" is not a thing: Redefining construct definitions and representation through a justice-oriented critical antiracist lens. *Educational Measurement: Issues and Practice, 40*(4), 82–90.

Rasooli, A., Zandi, H., & De Luca, C. (2018). Re-conceptualizing classroom assessment fairness: A systematic meta-ethnography of assessment literature and beyond. *Studies in Educational Evaluation, 56,* 164–181.

Taylor, C. (2022). *Culturally and socially responsible assessment: Theory, research, and practice.* Teachers College Press.

Wormeli, R. (2007). *Differentiation: From planning to practice, grades 6–12.* Stenhouse.

Wormeli, R. (2018). *Fair isn't always equal: Assessment and grading in the differentiated classroom* (2nd ed.). Stenhouse.

12

Designing Performance Tasks

What Are Performance Tasks?

Performance assessment is assessment of a process or product (or both) using observation and judgment. It has two parts: the *performance task* or tasks and a *rubric* or other scheme that organizes criteria upon which to base the observation and judgment. This chapter discusses how to design performance tasks. They can range from simple to complex, from short to long-term, and from individual to group. The key to designing the performance task is to consider how it would give evidence of the specific learning goals you want to assess. Chapter 13 discusses how to design rubrics. Taken together, Chapters 12 and 13 describe how to create and use performance assessments.

Why Are Performance Tasks Important?

Performance tasks help students get a clear idea of what they are learning—what it is they are supposed to know and be able to do. A task, more so than a test, helps students envision what the learning goal looks like. Some, although not all, performance tasks show students what applying knowledge looks like in a real-world setting. Further, performing a task requires active engagement, and active engagement helps many students with both motivation and learning. Performance tasks, especially those involving some student choice, are more likely to allow students to bring their own background and voice to bear on the task than do test items. Finally, performance tasks are necessary for assessing achievement of some complex standards that cannot be fully assessed with test questions.

How Do I Use Performance Tasks in My Teaching and Assessment?

The process for designing a performance task involves several steps:

- Identify the content to be assessed.
- Identify the thinking skills to be assessed.
- Draft a task with criteria to match the intended learning to be assessed.
- Check for a match between the draft task and intended content and thinking skills.
- Check that the requirements of the task do not add additional, irrelevant skills.
- Revise the task.

The process is not finished at this point; the next step is to use the criteria to create a rubric. Chapter 13 will address this step.

Matching the Cognitive Level and Difficulty of a Task with the Content and Thinking Skills to Be Assessed

Learning goals describe different kinds of outcomes. Students might be asked to learn to recall facts, understand concepts, apply knowledge to solve problems, analyze information, design and produce products, or perform a process. A test is an efficient way to assess recall of facts or understanding of concepts. Performance assessment is the most efficient way to assess student processes or products. Both performance assessments and tests can assess application of knowledge and analysis of information, depending on the particular learning outcomes and the specific questions and tasks used to assess them. Figure 12.1 shows recommendations for matching the cognitive level of a task with an assessment method, using both the cognitive process dimension of Bloom's taxonomy and Webb's Depth of Knowledge.

Once you have decided that you will use a performance task to assess a learning outcome, make sure the task matches the desired level. For example, if you want to assess whether students can analyze the imagery in a poem, the task should require analysis of imagery in a poem and not, for example, defining various kinds of imagery or filling in a worksheet about metaphors and similes.

FIGURE 12.1
**Recommendations for Matching Choice
of Assessment Method to Cognitive Level**

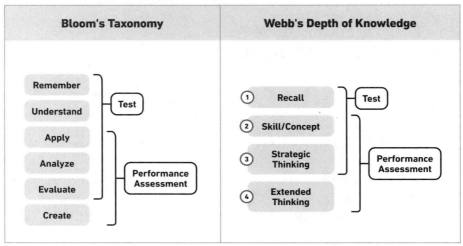

Task difficulty is a separate dimension from cognitive level. For example, there are easy recall items (1 + 1 = ?) and difficult recall items (recite *pi* to the first 100 digits). There are easy analysis questions ("Why did the Cat in the Hat want the house cleaned up before Mother got home?") and difficult analysis questions ("How did Hamlet feel about his mother Queen Gertrude?"). When you design a task, make sure what it asks students to do is at the appropriate level of difficulty for the standard and for the students who will take the assessment. Also leverage task design to encourage student involvement. For example, make sure the task requires of students as much voice and choice, opportunities for reflection and feedback, and appropriate use of technology as is feasible. If the task involves a real-world setting, make sure it is one with which your students are familiar.

Controlling Other Features of Performance Assessment Tasks: Length, Task Structure, and Group Work

Performance tasks can be long or short. Performance assessment can involve several tasks (e.g., take multiple measures over time of the height of the plant in a terrarium and amount of water and sunlight each day, prepare a graph of the plant's growth, present the results in a chart, and explain the meaning of the chart) or just one task. The length of the task and the number of tasks become important when you think of the sampling aspect of a performance task. For any given learning outcome, you could pose an almost infinite number of tasks. But because performance tasks take time, you may only select one or a few. How accurately does student performance on one task represent student standing in the whole learning domain of interest? The answer depends on the length, complexity, and exact nature of the task or tasks you use.

Performance tasks can be individual, or they can involve varying amounts of group work. If you use group work in performance tasks, be sure that the outcome you are assessing involves collaborative problem solving or something similar. Do not fall into the trap of asking a group to do a task and then taking the result as a measure of individual group members' knowledge or skills. For summative (graded) work, individual evidence is needed for individual grades, so be sure to design tasks that yield individual evidence of learning. In Chapter 18, we'll argue against "group grades," and the best way to solve that problem is to design performance tasks that give individual information. One way to do that, of course, is to simply use individual tasks. Another is to design a project that includes an element of group work for which students will receive formative feedback, with pauses for check-ins, and yet requires individual reflection and individual outcome measures. Figure 12.2 gives an example of a performance task that uses group work for formative assessment and individual products for grading.

FIGURE 12.2
Example of a Performance Task with Group Work for Formative Assessment and Individual Work for Grading

Task
Propose a new mascot for our school and facilitate schoolwide support for adopting your animal as the new mascot.

In Groups	Individually
• Develop a campaign for your chosen animal, including a short speech (to be read over the intercom during morning announcements) and posters for display around the school. • Conduct an election; then collect votes and tally the results on a spreadsheet. *Note:* Neither of these activities is formally scored, but group work is formatively assessed and feedback is provided.	• Develop an appropriate graphic display of the collected data to use in communicating the results of the mascot vote to the PTO executive board and the school principal. • Compose a letter to the principal and PTO board recommending which animal should be selected as the school's mascot. You must present your reasons, including your vote data display, to make your case. *Note:* Both of these individual activities are assessed with rubrics based on the respective standards: (1) display of data and (2) persuasive writing with evidence.

Source: From *Designing Authentic Performance Tasks and Projects* (p. 160), by J. McTighe, K. J. Doubet, and E. M. Carbaugh, 2020, ASCD. Copyright 2020 by ASCD.

One important feature of performance tasks is that they can vary in the amount of student choice or openness involved. For many complex learning outcomes, students need to be able to identify problems, design solutions, and present results without being told, cookbook-style, how to do that. Such a cookbook approach renders the task an assessment of students' ability to follow directions more than of their achievement of a complex learning outcome. For example, part of a science assessment might include writing a testable hypothesis and designing an experiment to test it rather than being given directions that included the hypothesis and experimental procedures. Figure 12.3 presents a framework for designing tasks with more and less openness in their structure. Whenever possible, at least one aspect of the task should be unstructured or guided. This gives students choices about their learning. Note that student choices should be related to the learning that is assessed—not, for example, to extraneous features like decorating the finished product.

Preparing Performance Tasks for Students

Figure 12.4 gives some examples of performance tasks that are both simple and complex and that assess processes or products. Prepare performance tasks for students by including complete directions, a time frame,

FIGURE 12.3
A Framework for Controlling the Amount of Structure in Performance Assessment Tasks

Task Feature	Less Structure ⟵⟶ More Structure		
	Not Provided	**Guided**	**Provided**
Identify problem, pose question, or define task.	Learner poses a question, problem, or task.	Teacher gives learner a selection of questions to choose from or to adapt.	Teacher provides the question, problem, or task.
Select and use strategies and materials for solving problem, answering question, or completing task.	Learner selects strategies and materials.	Teacher suggests strategies and materials for students to use or adapt.	Teacher gives learner strategies and materials.
Present solution, answer, performance, or final product.	Learner decides how to present solution, answer, performance, or final product.	Teacher suggests presentation methods for learner to use or adapt.	Teacher gives learner directions for presentation.

Source: From *How to Design Questions and Tasks to Assess Student Thinking* (p. 79), by S. M. Brookhart, 2014, ASCD. Copyright 2014 by ASCD.

FIGURE 12.4
Examples of Performance Assessment

	Processes	Products
Simple	• Make a capital A. • Count by 10s to 100. • Keyboard 50 words per minute.	• Write a story about a dog. • Make a model of the solar system. • Solve a math problem two different ways and then explain which method was more efficient and why.
Complex	• Use a variety of basketball skills to play a game of basketball. • Share your story and receive feedback by participating in Author's Chair. • Plan a one-week trip highlighting historical sites in your state.	• Interpret original source material and draw conclusions about a historical event, presenting the results in a written report. • Design, conduct, and report on a science experiment. • Design a mathematical model to inform and solve a problem. • Interview an elderly person about a time before you were born and compare their experience of the event with historical information from your textbook or other sources, presenting the results in a video.

the task(s) itself and any necessary materials, and the rubrics or other scoring scheme that contain the criteria you and the students should be looking for in their work. Check that the final performance task, as presented, does not require extra skills that are not related to the learning outcome (e.g., art skills for some presentation products, or extraordinary computer skills) and especially not skills that might cause a student to be mismeasured (e.g., requiring extremely shy students to perform in front of a large class).

How Do I Involve Students in Performance Tasks?

All performance tasks require students to *do* something, so by definition there is already some student involvement. The most important way to involve students in performance tasks is to make sure students have at least some choice in aspects of the performance task. The way to do that is to use the framework for controlling the amount of task structure in Figure 12.3.

Some performance tasks lend themselves to a lot of active student involvement. For example, this author once observed 5th graders, in groups, putting on skits for their classmates about the idea of taxation without representation. The characters were to be King George III, George Washington, a colonist, and a Native American. The lines each character spoke were to reflect their point of view. I was more impressed than I expected to be—I'll admit to being a bit skeptical about whether young children could carry this off or would just play costume drama. The dialogue was rich and showed surprising understanding about how different groups had different perspectives. This was a group task and received formative feedback.

What Are Some Common Misconceptions About Performance Tasks?

One common misconception about performance tasks is that they are always "authentic assessment," that is, always real-world tasks. Many performance tasks are, but many are not. For example, solving a complex math problem in two different ways (e.g., using a table and using equations), then explaining your reasoning and explaining which solution you preferred and why, is a pretty academic task—but it is a performance assessment.

Another misconception—I'm not sure how common—about performance tasks is that all students love them. In fact, some students who do well on tests prefer tests to performance tasks because they are quicker and (for them) take less effort. If you have a learning outcome that can be assessed with both a test and a performance assessment, try doing both, which will serve the goal of using multiple measures (see Chapter 11) and give you a richer picture of students' achievement on that outcome.

FOR FURTHER READING

Brookhart, S. (2014). *How to design questions and tasks to assess student thinking.* ASCD.

Brookhart, S. M. (2015). *Performance assessment: Showing what students know and can do.* Learning Sciences International.

Fisher, D., & Frey, N. (2014). *Checking for understanding: Formative assessment techniques for your classroom* (2nd ed.). ASCD.

McTighe, J., Doubet, K. J., & Carbaugh, E. M. (2020). *Designing authentic performance tasks and projects: Tools for meaningful learning and assessment.* ASCD.

Michaels, S., Shouse, A., & Schweingruber, H. (2008). *Ready, set, science!* National Academies Press.

13

Crafting Rubrics and Other Multi-Point Scoring

What Are Rubrics?

A rubric is composed of two parts: a set of criteria to apply to student work and descriptions of performance across a range of quality. They are commonly used for assessing students' work on performance tasks. Other multi-point scoring formats (checklists, rating scales, and point schemes) are also based on criteria but do not have performance level descriptions. The performance level descriptions make rubrics useful for both formative assessment (including self- and peer assessment) and summative assessment (grading), and for this reason the chapter recommends rubrics for use with performance tasks except in special circumstances.

Why Are Rubrics Important?

Rubrics are useful for assessing complex performances that require teacher judgment. They are an important tool in the formative learning process and an important tool connecting classroom formative and summative assessment because they can be used for teacher feedback, student self- and peer assessment during learning, and—subsequently—grading.

Rubrics organize the criteria and performance level descriptions into a useful format for both teachers and students. Organized, explicit criteria and performance level descriptions help make teacher judgment more reliable. Organized, explicit criteria and performance level descriptions also help students assess their own work. Students can see where they are now and what their work would look like if they improved it. Similarly, teachers can use rubrics to present organized feedback that focuses on the criteria.

How Do I Use Rubrics in My Teaching and Assessment?

First, create high-quality rubrics. You can write them yourself; you can locate, review, and revise rubrics from another source; or you can cocreate them with students. Then, use the rubrics in formative ways, for student self-assessment and teacher or peer feedback, and in grading. Figure 13.1 gives an example of a rubric for science laboratory reports. Students can use the rubric to monitor their work as they prepare their reports, and for formal or informal self- and peer assessment during learning. The teacher can use the same rubric for grading after the work is completed.

Create High-Quality Rubrics

Appropriate *criteria* are the foundation of high-quality rubrics. Criteria are appropriate when they name qualities in student work that give evidence of how well students are approaching the learning goal you are assessing. Appropriate criteria are definable and observable—you and your students will need to recognize these qualities when you see them. Criteria should name distinct aspects of the work, so that each criterion looks for something different, and together the criteria should form a set that completely describes what the desired learning looks like. In addition, you should be able to describe each criterion over a range of performance levels.

Performance level descriptions are the second hallmark of high-quality rubrics. Descriptions of what work looks like over the range of performance levels help students and teachers pinpoint a student's current status on a learning goal and identify what the student should do next. Those descriptions should do just that—describe what work at that level looks like. Rubrics that use evaluative words instead of descriptive ones (e.g., "good topic sentence") are not helpful because they beg the question of what makes the topic sentence good. Students who want to aim for a good topic sentence need a description of what one looks like. Of course, the descriptions need to be clear to the student, and the descriptions need to convey what distinguishes one level from another. Aim for parallel descriptions from one level to the next, to convey what changes in the elements of the description would be needed to move from one level to the next. Performance level

FIGURE 13.1
Science Laboratory Report Rubric

	4	**3**	**2**	**1**
Introduction— Stating Research Questions and Hypotheses	States a hypothesis that is based on research and/or sound reasoning and is testable. Report title reflects question or hypothesis.	States a hypothesis that is based on research and/or sound reasoning and is testable. Report title may not reflect the question or hypothesis.	States a hypothesis, although basis for the hypothesis is not clear or hypothesis is not testable. Report title may not reflect the question or hypothesis.	Does not state a hypothesis. Introduction may be a general statement of the topic or the assignment, or may be missing or unclear.
Procedure— Designing the Experiment	Procedure includes a very detailed description or step-by-step list of how the experiment was performed. All steps are included.	Procedure includes a very detailed description or step-by-step list of how the experiment was performed; however, not all steps are included.	Description or step-by-step list of how the experiment was performed is vague and experiment would be hard for someone else to duplicate.	Description is unclear, and experiment could not be repeated because of lack of description.
Results— Collecting Data	Results and data are accurately recorded, organized so that it is easy for the reader to see trends. All appropriate labels are included.	Results are clear and labeled. Trends are not obvious.	Results are unclear, missing labels, and trends are not obvious at all.	Results may be present but too disorganized or poorly recorded to make sense of.
Analyzing Data	The data and observations are analyzed accurately. Trends are noted. Enough data were taken to establish conclusion.	Analysis is somewhat lacking in insight. There is enough data, although additional data would be more powerful.	Analysis is lacking in insight. Not enough data were gathered to establish trends, or analysis does not follow the data.	Analysis is inaccurate and based on insufficient data.
Interpreting Results and Drawing Conclusions	Summarizes data used to draw logical conclusions about hypothesis. Discusses real-world applications of findings.	Summarizes data used to draw conclusions about hypothesis. Some logic or real-world application may be unclear.	Conclusions about hypothesis are not derived from data. Some logic or real-world application may be unclear.	No conclusions about hypothesis are evident. Logic and application of findings are missing.

Source: From *How to Create and Use Rubrics for Formative Assessment and Grading* (pp. 85–86), by S. M. Brookhart, ASCD. Copyright 2013 by ASCD.

descriptions should cover the whole range of performance, from very poor to exemplary, even if the teacher does not expect to find any students who are, for example, very poor. The continuum itself helps communicate what the criterion means. Finally, make sure that the description of proficient or acceptable performance, at whatever level you set it, conveys proficiency and not perfection.

The *number of levels* is less important than the clarity of the performance level descriptions. There should never be more levels than you can make clear distinctions in performance. It is often useful to use the same number of levels that you will ultimately need for grading and reporting, to save the trouble and potential confusion of making decision rules for converting the rubric scale at grading time. Levels can be named as grade categories (e.g., ABCDF, Advanced Proficient Novice), or numbered (4,3,2,1) or named in student-friendly terms with text (e.g., Wow, Almost There, Not Yet) or graphics.

No one layout or format is recommended for rubrics. Often, rubrics are arranged in chart form with criteria naming the rows and performance levels naming the columns. Columns can be arranged from low to high, which has the advantage of reading left to right, or high to low, which has the advantage of putting the description of the high-quality work students will be aiming for next to the name of the criterion (as, e.g., in Figure 13.1). Sometimes, the criteria name the columns and the performance level descriptions name the rows (as in Figure 13.2).

Use Rubrics for Formative Assessment and Grading

Teachers can incorporate rubrics into their instruction, checking for student understanding of the criteria and performance level descriptions as they share learning targets. Teachers can then base formative feedback on the rubrics, and have students base self- and peer assessment on the rubrics as well. After students have had an opportunity to practice, teachers can use the same rubrics for grading final work. The section "How Do I Involve Students in Rubrics?" below presents various strategies for doing this.

For this very reason, that using rubrics involves students, it is very effective to use general rubrics that can be applied to more than one task in a domain (e.g., math problem-solving rubrics, narrative writing rubrics, science lab rubrics) rather than task-specific rubrics that can be used with one assignment only (e.g., problem-solving rubrics that refer to specific decisions required to do just the problems in question). Students learn to work with the criteria and can use them to generalize skills, for example, learning that all effective problem solving exhibits certain criteria.

FIGURE 13.2
Teacher's Rubric for Written Projects

	Content	Organization	Written Language	Visuals
4	The thesis is clear. A large amount and variety of material and evidence support the thesis. All material is relevant. This material includes details. Information is accurate. Appropriate sources were consulted.	Information is clearly and explicitly related to the point(s) the material is intended to support. Information is organized in a logical manner and is presented concisely. Flow is good. Introductions, transitions, and other connecting material take the listener/reader along.	There are few errors of grammar and usage; any minor errors do not interfere with meaning. Language style and word choice are highly effective and enhance meaning. Style and word choice are appropriate to the project.	Graphics, props, constructions, or multimedia successfully fulfill the purpose of the assignment. Material is clearly connected to the points to be made. Points would not have been as clearly made without the materials. Use of materials is varied and appropriate. Use of materials is original and captures the audience's or reader's attention.
3	The thesis is clear. An adequate amount of material and evidence supports the thesis. Most material is relevant. This material includes details. Information is mostly accurate; any inaccuracies are minor and do not interfere with the points made. Appropriate sources were consulted.	Information is clearly related to the point(s) the material is intended to support, although not all connections may be explained. Information is organized in a logical manner. Flow is adequate. Introductions, transitions, and other connecting material take the listener/reader along for the most part. Any abrupt transitions do not interfere with intended meaning.	Some errors of grammar and usage are present; errors do not interfere with meaning. Language style and word choice are for the most part effective and appropriate to the project.	Graphics, props, constructions, or multimedia fulfill the purpose of the assignment. Material illustrates the points to be made. Use of materials is varied and appropriate. Use of materials is somewhat original.
2	The thesis may be somewhat unclear. Some material and evidence support the thesis. Some of the material is relevant, and some is not. Details are lacking. Information may include some inaccuracies. At least some sources are appropriate.	Some of the information is related to the point(s) the material is intended to support, but connections are not explained. Information is not entirely organized in a logical manner, although some structure is apparent. Flow is choppy. Introductions, transitions, and other connecting material may be lacking or unsuccessful.	Major errors of grammar and usage begin to interfere with meaning. Language style and word choice are simple, bland, or otherwise not very effective or not entirely appropriate.	Graphics, props, constructions, or multimedia are not entirely connected to the purpose of the assignment. Not all material illustrates the points to be made. Use of materials is appropriate but lacks originality.

(continued)

FIGURE 13.2
Teacher's Rubric for Written Projects (*continued*)

	Content	Organization	Written Language	Visuals
1.	The thesis is not clear. Much of the material may be irrelevant to the overall topic or inaccurate. Details are lacking. Appropriate sources were not consulted.	Information is not related to the point(s) the material is intended to support. Information is not organized in a logical manner. Material does not flow. Information is presented as a sequence of unrelated material.	Major errors of grammar and usage make meaning unclear. Language style and word choice are ineffective and/or inappropriate.	Graphics, props, constructions, or multimedia are not connected to the purpose of the assignment. Material does not illustrate the points to be made (or there are no points made). Materials are not relevant, appropriate, or original.

Source: From *How to Give Effective Feedback to Your Students* (2nd ed.) (pp. 89–90), by S. M. Brookhart, 2017, ASCD. Copyright 2017 by ASCD.

Rubrics can also be described as analytic or holistic. Analytic rubrics consider each criterion separately and are good for feedback and student self-assessment. Holistic rubrics still use criteria, but they consider them simultaneously. Analytic, general rubrics, as described above and illustrated in Figures 13.1 and 13.2, are best for most classroom purposes. If a teacher is not going to give feedback and students are not going to use the rubric, holistic, task-specific rubrics typically make for faster scoring, but those situations are rare, for example, grading essays on a final examination.

Distinguish Rubrics from Other Scoring Schemes

For simple skills, sometimes a *checklist* is better than a rubric. A checklist has criteria but no performance level descriptions. Checklists assess each criterion with a yes/no or present/absent decision (e.g., My sentence starts with a capital, ends with a period, and expresses a complete thought). Checklists also work well for helping students follow directions and can be used in addition to the rubrics that will assess the learning evidence from the assignment.

Some people use a checklist-style version of rubrics they call "single-point rubrics." Statements of performance that combine aspects of criteria and the performance level description for proficient work are listed down the middle of a chart, and blank space is provided on each side to describe performance that is better or worse than the description as a form of feedback. Despite the name, single-point rubrics are not really rubrics, because they don't have complete performance level descriptions. They are better described as checklists.

A *rating scale* is another assessment tool that has criteria but no performance level descriptions. Rather, the performance levels are coded into scales, typically either evaluative scales or frequency scales. Evaluative scales (e.g., Excellent, Good, Fair, Poor or 5,4,3,2,1) are not very helpful for learning, because they don't convey any information about what is "excellent" or how a student with a "3" might improve their work to a "4." Frequency scales (e.g., Always, Often, Sometimes, Never) are useful for evaluating behavior, including learning skills behavior (works collaboratively with peers, does homework, brings a pencil to class, and so on). Frequency scales are not recommended for assessing content learning.

For essay questions or show-the-work math problems on tests, sometimes a *point scheme* is helpful for grading. For example, a student gets one point for understanding the problem, one point for writing an equation, one point for correctly solving the equation, and one point for labeling the answer.

All of these other scoring schemes are appropriate sometimes and can be part of a teacher's assessment repertoire and used in limited, special circumstances. As this chapter has shown, however, rubrics are more versatile and, especially, are particularly useful for connecting formative assessment during learning and summative assessment for grading. Because of their usefulness for formative assessment, rubrics are also particularly suited for involving students.

How Do I Involve Students in Rubrics?

You can use rubrics to involve students in their own assessment in all phases of the formative learning cycle: Where am I going? Where am I now? Where to next?

Where Am I Going?

Rubrics help clarify the learning goal for students. Working with the criteria for good work shows them what good work looks like, that is, what they're aiming to know and be able to do. Strategies to use rubrics at the time an assignment is introduced include the following.

Ask students to pose questions. When you first distribute a rubric, ask students to review it—individually or in pairs or groups—and ask questions about specific words or phrases in the rubric. For example, the Written Project Rubric in Figure 13.2 might be distributed at the time the project is assigned. Students could review the rubric and ask questions.

Ask students to restate the rubric in their own words. Restating something in one's own words is a classic comprehension activity. This will let you and the students know how well they understand the criteria. This activity is especially useful for a clear but lengthy rubric like the Written Project Rubric in Figure 13.2. Students could construct their own version of this rubric using their own voice.

Have students sort work samples into three piles: high, medium, and low quality. Before students receive the rubric, have small groups sort sample work into three piles and be prepared to explain why they placed each work sample where they did. Then, when they receive the rubric, have them compare their analysis with the criteria on the rubric.

Cocreate rubrics with students. Use the previous sorting strategy. Instead of giving students a rubric afterward, have them codify and collect their criteria using cards, sticky notes, chart paper, or a bulletin board or whiteboard app. Then with the class, group like criteria together, eliminate duplication, and finalize a student-created set of criteria for use in a rubric. You can stop there and write the performance level descriptions yourself. If the rubric is a general one that will be used many times, it may be worth the time to have the students write the performance level descriptions.

Where Am I Now?

Rubrics can guide work during learning. Typically, student involvement in this process is through either self- or peer assessment.

Self-assessment: matching work during learning. As students work, call for periodic reflection breaks where students apply the criteria and performance level descriptions to their own work as they are creating it. Do not assume that self-assessment comes naturally; rather, teach students how to do it by modeling and by giving feedback on the quality of their self-reflections.

Peer coaching. Instead of periodic self-reflection, have students pair up to do their reflection comparing emerging work with the rubric. Again, teach students how to do this. They should concentrate on the work, not their peer personally. Teach them to apply criteria and performance level descriptions to the work by finding evidence in the work that links to the descriptions.

Where to Next?

When students reach a good stopping place, for example, when they have finished a first draft of writing or a project, more formal self- and peer assessment is possible.

Formal self- or peer assessment. Whether individually or with a peer, students apply the rubric to the work and produce written (or, for young students, oral) feedback. A version of this strategy is to use highlighters to highlight a statement in the rubric (e.g., "models the problem using an equation") and then use the same color to highlight the evidence in the work (e.g., highlights the equation that modeled the problem).

Self-tracking. When the same rubric is used over and over again (e.g., some types of writing rubrics or a math problem-solving rubric), students can keep a graph or chart that shows their progress on successive assessments using the rubric.

What Are Some Common Misconceptions About Rubrics?

Some teachers think that rubrics should include directions for the assignment (e.g., has four pictures, work is neatly done). This can be tempting, in the short run, because it can force students to follow directions or lose points in their grade. However, the result is mismeasurement of student achievement. A student could do well on such a rubric but have only surface-level understanding of the learning goal. The criteria on a rubric should be qualities that indicate student learning, not compliance with directions. Use another strategy for that; for example, use a directions checklist and have students check each other's work before turning it in.

Some teachers think that the specificity involved in counting (e.g., persuasive writing has four supporting reasons, has three or fewer grammar errors) makes rubrics more precise. In fact, just the opposite is true. What makes student reasoning persuasive, for example, is not the number of them, but how relevant they are to the argument, how compelling they are to the reader, and so on. Three silly reasons are not better than two important and well-explained reasons. Again, this misconception can lead to mismeasuring student achievement and rewarding surface-level learning.

FOR FURTHER READING

Brookhart, S. M. (2013). *How to create and use rubrics for formative assessment and grading.* ASCD.

Brookhart, S. M. (2017). *How to give effective feedback to your students* (2nd ed.). ASCD.

Dueck, M. (2021). *Giving students a say: Smarter assessment practices to empower and engage.* ASCD.

McTighe, J., & Frontier, T. (2022). How to provide better feedback through rubrics. *Educational Leadership, 79*(7), 17–23. https://www.ascd.org/el/articles/how-to-provide-better-feedback-through-rubrics

14

Designing Classroom Tests

What Are Classroom Tests?

Classroom tests are probably the most common summative (graded) assessment method in use. The classroom tests discussed in this chapter are conventional teacher-created or teacher-selected classroom tests. They are often administered as paper-and-pencil exercises, although increasingly there are apps where teachers can create classroom tests for students to take using their devices. This chapter does not discuss computer-based tests designed outside the classroom and administered by computer-learning software, although some of the same principles apply. The classroom tests described in this chapter are teacher-created, typically in one of two ways. The teacher may create the test herself or with colleagues who also teach the same material. Or, the teacher may select a test, for example, a unit test that comes with a textbook or other curriculum materials she is using; however, in this case, she would review the test to make sure it assesses exactly what is needed for her purposes. If not, she can and should modify it before using it with students.

Why Are Classroom Tests Important?

Classroom tests are well suited to certain assessment purposes. For standards or portions of standards where the learning goal involves knowledge, especially factual and conceptual knowledge, and even some procedural knowledge, classroom tests allow you to get a large sample of student responses (many questions take only a minute or less for students to answer) so you can cover the domain of learning more thoroughly than with fewer, longer assessment tasks. Where the learning goal involves student cognition at the Bloom's taxonomy levels of Remember, Understand, or Apply, and sometimes Analyze (or Webb's Depth of Knowledge levels 1, 2, and sometimes 3), classroom tests allow you to sample more of the domain of learning than fewer, longer performance assessment tasks. Covering more of the domain of learning allows you to have more confidence in a student's test result as a valid indicator of the learning goal.

A large number of learning goals, therefore, can be assessed effectively and efficiently with a classroom test. The key is to begin with a very clear description of the learning goal to be assessed, so you know when a test is an effective assessment or when a performance assessment would be a better match, for example, for learning goals at Bloom's Evaluate or Create levels of thinking or Webb's DOK 4 (Extended Thinking) level.

How Do I Use Classroom Tests in My Teaching and Assessment?

Be aware that you wouldn't start planning for one test without reference to a larger assessment plan, which typically is part of your school or department's curriculum map, or whatever organizing tool is used. This larger assessment plan should tell you what assessment(s) are needed for what standards or learning goals. When a test is part of that assessment plan, you will need to create it or review and perhaps modify a test from your teaching materials. This chapter starts at that point.

First, determine the test's purpose and the specific learning goal(s) the test will assess. Will you use it for grading? Will students use the results formatively? Explicitly state the learning goal(s) to be assessed and identify the content knowledge and thinking skills in that domain of learning. Stop and take stock. Is a test appropriate for all the learning goals, or do some of them need to be assessed with a performance assessment? It is possible, for example, to have a culminating assessment in a unit that consists of both a classroom test and a performance assessment.

Second, once you have identified the learning goals you will be assessing with the test alone, create a test plan, sometimes called a test blueprint or a table of specifications. There are many ways to do this. This chapter shows a few of them. The important goal for any test plan is to make sure you and the students know what the final test score represents. Consider, for example, two teachers who each make their own test for a unit on plants without a test plan. One teacher's test consists mostly of terms for students to identify and define (vascular and nonvascular plants, gymnosperm, angiosperm, etc.). One teacher's test consists mostly of applied questions about observing and categorizing plants, designing a garden, and so on. Both tests yield percentage-based scores that are translated into grades (*A*, *B*, *C*, *D*, *F*). Those scores and grades mean very different things about what students know and how they think about plants. Neither teacher's test results represent the learning goals from the unit on plants; each one leaves something out.

A test plan will help you think through the best distribution of test questions to represent intended learning goals. It will help you decide how to proportion the score so that the whole represents the unit goals, and this in turn will help you decide what kind of test questions you can use. If you are working in a standards-based school where grading and reporting is done by standard, a test plan will help you organize your test questions into sections that can be separately scored and assessed by standard.

There are many ways to make a test plan. I illustrate two of them here. Test plans are typically in chart or list form. No matter what format is used, test plans need to do the following:

- Specify the learning goal that a test question or questions will assess, in terms of both content and cognitive level.
- Specify how many points and what portion of the total score each learning goal receives.

Additional things that test plans can and often do include the following:

- Specify how many questions for each learning goal.
- Specify how many points per question for each learning goal.

Figure 14.1 shows a common kind of test blueprint in chart form for a middle school unit on cells. The unit has four learning goals: (1) understand that living things are made of cells, which in turn are made up of parts called organelles; (2) distinguish living from nonliving things; (3) identify basic parts of a cell and their functions; (4) develop a model of a cell and use it to explain the functions of the cell as a whole and its parts. The teacher determines that the first three learning goals can be assessed with a classroom test, and the fourth learning goal (develop a model and explain it) requires a performance assessment. She plans two culminating assessments for her unit, the classroom test and a performance assessment. The blueprint in Figure 14.1 is the blueprint for the test.

FIGURE 14.1
**Test Plan for a Middle School Classroom Test on Cells,
Organized by Learning Goals and Level of Thinking**

Learning Goal	Remember	Understand	Apply	Total
Understand living things are made of cells	2	4		6 (20%)
Distinguish living things from nonliving things	2		4	6 (20%)
Identify basic parts of a cell and their functions	6	6	6	18 (60%)
Total	10 (33%)	10 (33%)	10 (33%)	30 (100%)

The first column of the blueprint shows the learning goals. Each goal will be assessed with questions at the Remember, Understand, or Apply level of Bloom's taxonomy. Other ways of categorizing cognitive level could be used, for example, Webb's Depth of Knowledge or a simple dichotomy of Recall and Higher-Order Thinking. As an example, the chart shows that two points are planned at the Remember (recall) level to assess understanding that living things are made of cells. This could be two multiple-choice questions or two true-false questions of one point each, or one two-point short answer question. No matter the format, the questions are planned to assess recall. In addition, the chart shows there are four points planned for questions at the Understand (comprehension) level. Again, that could be four one-point questions, two two-point questions, one four-point question, or some combination, but no matter the format the questions are planned to assess comprehension.

The totals for both rows and columns are also an important part of the test plan. Figure 14.1 shows that a 30-point test is planned. It also shows that the learning reflected in the total test score, if one is used, represents recall, comprehension, and application in equal measure. It also shows that more of the test score represents identifying basic parts of a cell and their functions than the other two learning goals. That proportion represents a teacher decision about the complexity and importance of that specific learning goal relative to the others. A test plan is an aid to making those kinds of decisions. When you are drafting your chart, it is easy to change the numbers to reflect your thinking about the relative weights you want to assign to different content or levels of thinking—much easier than rewriting questions later on. When you use a test plan, by the time you get to writing the questions you know what kind and how many you need.

Note two other things about the construction of this type of test plan. You do not need to list every possible cognitive level. In this example, only three of Bloom's taxonomy levels (Remember, Understand, Apply) are listed. There is no need for columns for Analyze, Evaluate, or Create because the test will not have any questions at those levels. Similarly, you do not need to put numbers in every cell. Only those cells that represent the content and level of thinking of actual questions you plan for the test will be filled.

The test plan does *not* say anything about the relative weight of these three learning goals to the fourth one, developing a model, that has been removed from the test and assessed with a performance assessment. That information will surface in the relative weighting the teacher gives to the test and performance assessment in determining the final unit grade.

Figure 14.2 shows another way of organizing a test plan for the same unit test. Again, the first column states the learning goals, because they are the basis for the assessment. In this format, the columns are arranged to emphasize the number and type of items and their point value. What is lost in this format is a total for each cognitive level. What is gained is a checklist-style presentation of the kind of test questions you need to write. You can

FIGURE 14.2
Test Plan for a Middle School Classroom Test on Cells, Organized by Learning Goals and Item Specifications

Learning Goal	Item Type	Number of Items	Number of Points
Understand living things are made of cells	Remember 2 MC Understand 2 SA	4	6
Distinguish living things from nonliving things	Remember 2 MC Apply 2 SA	4	6
Identify basic parts of a cell and their functions	Remember 6 MC Understand 6 MC Apply 3 SA	15	18
Total	MC = 16 SA = 7	23	30

MC = multiple choice, 1 point each
SA = short answer, 2 points each

also do a hybrid format by using the chart style from Figure 14.1 and adding information about item types and numbers into the cells.

Test questions can be grouped into two general categories, selected response (see Chapter 15) and constructed response (see Chapter 16). In this chapter, we focus on the plan or design for the classroom test. Once you have a design you are satisfied with, you can write the test using the suggestions in those chapters. You will find it's much easier to write test questions once you have a plan (e.g., "I need three multistep word problems that use both addition and multiplication") than without one ("I need to write some math problems").

Once you have a test plan, give some thought to the organization of the test. Even if your school uses traditional grading, it is recommended that you organize your test questions by standard or learning goal. Some teachers organize their classroom tests by format (e.g., a section of multiple choice, a section of true-false, a section of short written responses), but organizing by content makes more sense for students and, for teachers, allows standards- or learning-goal-based interpretations (no matter what sort of reporting system you use), which helps with student self-reflection and with teachers' further instructional decisions. Of course, that doesn't mean your test should be a jumble of different items that confuse students or need repeated, long directions. Often, each learning goal can be assessed with one or two question formats.

For small, quiz-sized tests, a simple list may suffice for a test plan. For example, suppose your 3rd graders had been working on using commas in sentences, and you wanted to use a quiz to check that students could use commas in lists, to separate clauses in a sentence, and to set off transition words, names, and parts of sentences that are not necessary to meaning. Your quiz would be in the form of sentences for the students to punctuate. They would all require thinking at the Application level (solving problems that have one right answer). You might make a simple list to say you were going to write two sentences that needed commas in lists, two sentences that needed commas to separate clauses, two sentences that needed commas to set off transition words or names, and two sentences that needed commas to set off nonessential information.

Third, write the test. Write the selected response or constructed response questions to match the test plan. Use Chapters 15 and 16 to help you. Then, write clear directions that tell students how they should respond to the questions in each section of the test. Even for directions that might seem obvious (e.g., "Choose the best answer by circling the letter of your choice"), write directions. Or, for younger students or any student who cannot read well, plan how you will give oral directions. Most students could probably figure out some of these things, but that's not their job, it's yours. Chapters 15 and 16 have more detailed suggestions about directions for different test question formats.

Finally, if you need to create a makeup test for a student who has been absent, or write a similar test for next year, use the same test plan. Write different items to the same specifications, and you will have a somewhat parallel measure that you can use. The reason for using another test instead of, for example, just giving your absentee student the same one is that once knowledge and comprehension-level questions are known to students, they no longer represent the domain of knowledge in the same way. Consider, for example, that a student was absent during that unit test on plants. When they return to school, it is likely that their classmates will have shared at least some of the material (e.g., "angiosperm" was on the test, but "gymnosperm" wasn't). Studying for the test, for the absentee, is no longer studying the whole domain of learning, but just studying the bits of it they know to be on the test. The score may be inflated because of that—or it may not be; the point is that you no longer know what it means. Test scores that can't be interpreted are useless.

How Do I Involve Students in Classroom Tests?

Studying for classroom tests is part of the process of learning. Contrary to popular belief, it's not the only part of testing that contributes to long-term learning—taking the test actually aids learning as well—but studying is definitely important. For older students, you can share your test plan when you assign the test, as an aid to studying. Do not share the actual test questions, just the plan, so that students will know, for example, that there will be 5 points worth of questions about this learning goal, 10 about that one, and so on, and something about what kinds of questions those might be.

Another way to use the test plan with students is to have them write review questions to it. For example, students might write multiple-choice questions and short essay questions that they think fit a test plan you have shared, and then use them in class for review. The review can include a self-reflection, or a game, or a small-group activity, for example. This gives students practice with questions in the learning domain, and practice envisioning what competence on the learning targets looks like. A clearer idea of the learning domain, envisioned in terms of test questions, can help students study more effectively.

For younger students, your test plan will typically be very brief, and you can structure review around it without giving students the plan. For example, if your 3rd graders finished a math unit on understanding place value and properties of operations, your test blueprint might call for some questions on rounding whole numbers to the nearest 10 or 100, adding and subtracting within 1000 using strategies based on place value, and multiplying one-digit whole numbers by multiples of 10 using strategies based on place value. Each of those types of problems could form the basis for a learning center to which students could circulate for review in any of the ways you use learning centers in your classroom.

What Are Some Common Misconceptions About Classroom Tests?

Several misconceptions about classroom tests are really reactions to poor classroom tests. One of these misconceptions is that "classroom test" means a multiple-choice test. A corollary of that is the misconception that tests only test recall of information, not student thinking. In fact, as this chapter has shown, poorly planned tests may do this, but effectively planned tests should not. Effectively planned tests should help students clarify their learning targets—yes, even at the end of a unit, it's still possible to develop a clearer idea of what has been learned—and show them what kinds of questions they can answer.

Another misconception some teachers have is that students hate tests. In fact, some students like tests better than performance assessments because they are quicker. These students tend to be students who do well on tests, of course. When you ask students "how much work" they need to do for an assessment, they will often answer in terms of the amount of time they need to spend.

Finally, an especially pernicious misconception is that students' tests should be written in the format of the state test, as test preparation. It is true that students need practice with question formats they will be asked to use. Giving students some practice at those formats is part of a teacher's responsibility. However, it does not follow that classroom tests, in general, should look like state accountability tests. As this chapter shows, classroom tests should look like an embodiment of the learning goal(s) they are meant to assess, using the most appropriate format to get the soundest and most representative information about student achievement on those goals.

FOR FURTHER READING

Brookhart, S. M. (2014). *How to design questions and tasks to assess student thinking.* ASCD.

Brookhart, S. M., & Nitko, A. J. (2019). *Educational assessment of students* (8th ed.). Pearson.

Chappuis, J., & Stiggins, R. (2020). *Classroom assessment for student learning: Doing it right—using it well* (3rd ed.). Pearson.

15

Writing Selected Response Test Questions

What Are Selected Response Test Questions?

Selected response test questions are test items for which students choose an answer as their response. (In this book, "test question" and "test item" are used synonymously.) Selected response test questions include multiple-choice, true-false, and matching items and fill-in-the-blank items that have a word bank. These test item formats are very common in both teacher-created and publisher-created tests. If done well and used wisely, they can provide information about a range of learning goals, to both students and teachers.

Why Are Selected Response Test Questions Important?

Selected response items are easy to score and assess certain learning goals efficiently. All types of selected response items can assess learning goals that focus on recall of facts and concepts. Multiple-choice and true-false items can also assess learning goals that focus on understanding and application of facts and concepts. Because students typically do not need a long time to respond to selected response items, a test can include more questions. More questions means the test can sample a larger portion of the domain of learning represented by the learning goal, which in turn gives you more confidence that students' results on the test are representative of their learning in the whole domain.

How Do I Use Selected Response Test Questions in My Teaching and Assessment?

Two major principles underlie the creation of sound tests that yield interpretable and actionable results. First, the test should include questions that require students to use the content knowledge and level of thinking implicated in the learning goals you intend to assess. Chapter 14 showed how to plan for that for the test as a whole. This chapter shows how to write individual test items that align to intended content and thinking skills while avoiding ambiguity or the kind of gaming that poor items have inadvertently trained test-wise students to do. For example, the test-wise truism "the longest answer is always correct" doesn't work if all the choices are about the same length. Second, no test item should require students to use other, irrelevant knowledge and skills in their responses. If it does, the test is not measuring only the learning goals, and the test results are not interpretable. When you write a test—whether you use selected response questions, constructed response questions, or some of each—check for those two things, plus a third, that the number and point value of your test items fits your test plan.

You can use those three points as a checklist for effective test items:

- Elicit content and thinking skills required by the learning goal you intend to assess.
- Do not require irrelevant content and thinking skills.
- Match your test plan in terms of number and point value.

In addition to these three important conceptual principles about the content of the test questions, three simple writing principles will help you write clear items that yield interpretable results. Effectively written selected response items should do the following:

- Use language that is as simple and straightforward as possible.
- Avoid wording that is identical to the textbook or other materials.
- Avoid language that gives a clue to the answer of this or another question.

Using simple, straightforward language will ensure that, to the extent possible, your test questions are not measuring students' ability to read. If possible, try writing test items at a reading level one or two grades below the grade level you are testing—in content areas other than reading, of course. This doesn't mean you should avoid content-relevant vocabulary. Important content vocabulary that has been part of the learning goal can be used. Avoiding textbook wording helps keep the language simple, and it also avoids a common problem. Some students will think anything that sounds like something from their textbook will necessarily be true or important, whether it is or not. For this reason, avoid copying from a textbook or other class materials directly into your test questions. Instead, paraphrase in simple language.

Finally, because each item contributes a point(s) to the test's total score, each item should be independent. Clues can crop up in a set of test items, for example, if one item refers to mercury as a metal and another item asks what type of element mercury is. Such clues render the point from the second item meaningless—or at least, it measures clever reading rather than understanding of elements. Similarly, grammar and other clues can sometimes operate within an item, for example, when the correct response begins with a vowel and the item uses "an." Again, the point for a correct item is meaningless—does a correct answer indicate the student knows a concept or knows which answer started with a vowel?

Beyond these general principles that apply to all test questions, Figure 15.1 summarizes specific guidelines for creating each item format. The purpose of all these suggestions is to increase the likelihood of students responding to the question as you intended, using the content knowledge and thinking skills from their learning goals and not getting tripped up by irrelevant factors or confused by unclear wording.

Fill-in-the-Blank Items

Fill-in-the-blank items, as the name implies, are questions with a blank afterward or statements with a blank inside them. If fill-in-the-blank items are accompanied by a word bank from which students can choose their response, they function as selected-response items. If there is no word bank, the guidelines discussed here still apply, and the fill-in item is the simplest version of a constructed response item. In addition to the general conceptual and language concerns that all test items share, the guidelines for fill-in-the-blank items in Figure 15.1 help ensure that students respond to the substance of the item and a point for a correct answer indicates student learning, not students' logical, grammatical, or reading skills.

Fill-in items that are written as questions are typically clearer than items that have a blank in a declarative sentence. In addition, there should

FIGURE 15.1
Guidelines for Writing Different Selected Response Test Questions

---

Fill-in-the-Blank Items
- Are written as questions if possible.
- Have a single correct answer that assesses an important idea.
- Have one or, at most, two blank(s) at or near the end of the item.
- Have all blanks the same length.

True-False Items
- Have a single correct answer that assesses an important idea.
- Focus on one important concept.
- Are unquestionably either true or false.
- Are all about the same length.

Matching Items
- Give directions about the basis for matching.
- Are grouped into exercises of fewer than 10 items.
- Are homogeneous in content within an exercise.
- Place longer phrases in the premises (the items) and shorter ones in the responses.
- Order the responses (e.g., alphabetically, logically).
- Make sure that process of elimination cannot be used for answering.

Multiple-Choice Items
- Have stems that ask or imply a question.
- Have a single correct or best answer choice.
- Have choices that are all plausible to a student who does not know the content.
- Have distractors that represent common misconceptions if possible.
- Avoid "all of the above" and use "none of the above" sparingly.

---

be a single correct answer that assesses an idea important to the learning goal you are intending to assess. For example, consider "The author of *War and Peace* was _____." Several answers are possible: Leo Tolstoy, a Russian, a historian and philosopher, and so on. A direct question ("Who was the author of *War and Peace*?") is clearer and more likely to elicit from students the author's name if they know it. Without the direct question, even some trivial answers are possible (e.g., "a novelist"). That might not be a good answer, but you would be hard pressed to tell a student that it was wrong.

Typically, one blank is best, because that ensures that the fill-in item is assessing one thing. Occasionally, two blanks are possible for some learning goals, for example, "Hydrogen is composed of which two atomic particles?" (a proton and an electron). In either case, the blank should be at or near the end of the item to prevent students who know the answer from having to read the item twice. For example, to answer "_____ was a leading spokesperson for the U.S. civil rights movement in the mid-20th century," when the student encounters the blank, they do not know what is needed to fill it

(Martin Luther King Jr.). They need to read to the end, then circle back to answer, wasting time and cognitive resources. When phrased as a question with the blank at the end ("Who was a leading spokesperson for the U.S. civil rights movement in the mid-20th century?" _____), students can answer when they get to the blank without backtracking and potentially getting lost.

All the blanks in a fill-in exercise should be the same length. The length of the blank should not be a clue to the answer, implying a longer or a shorter word. Other clues to do with the visual arrangement of the blanks, for example, two blanks together to clue students to an answer like "New York," are also poor form. The problem is that interpreting blanks is not part of the learning goal. The clue may help students get a point, but you won't know what the point means. I have heard teachers say that they use such visual clues to help their students with learning disabilities score points. The same reasoning applies, though. The student should be tested on the content, not their knowledge of whether words are long or short, or are composed of two words, or whatever. "Getting points" is not the purpose, and drawing suggestive blanks is not an appropriate accommodation or modification of a test.

True-False Items

True-false items are test questions in the form of a statement students evaluate as true or false. True and False are the answer choices. Other dichotomous selected response items work like true-false questions, for example, items where the student must select yes/no or correct/incorrect as the answer. If carefully constructed, true-false items can assess recall of course, but they can also assess making predictions, generalizations, or comparisons, or evaluating evidence, conditions, relations, or procedures—in short, true-false items can assess learning goals at several different cognitive levels. As for all test items, the key is that the response the item elicits from students represents knowledge or reasoning that matches the intended learning goal.

Similar to fill-in items and for the same reasons, true-false items should have a single correct answer that assesses an important aspect of the learning goal to be assessed. Each item should focus on one important concept. If there are two concepts in the statement, you can't tell if a correct answer means the student knows one or both of them. For example, consider the item "George Washington was a delegate to the Continental Congress and the first president of the United States" (true). A student might get the question correct on the basis of "first president" without knowing about the Continental Congress, although a correct answer implies the student knows both things.

True-false items should be either definitely true or definitely false—not just true or false most of the time. Opinions can be tested with true-false items, but if they are, the source of the opinion should be cited. For example, "The best solution to the problem of homelessness is to build more affordable housing" is a statement that can be argued as true or false. The statement, "According to the National Alliance to End Homelessness, the best solution to the problem of homelessness is to build more affordable housing," however, is a true statement.

Sometimes, in order to make true statements definitely true, people write lots of qualifiers into the statement. That can result in the true statements being longer than the false statements, and test-wise students may pick up on that. When you write a true-false exercise, make sure all the true statements represent roughly the same length as the false statements. Getting a true-false item correct should mean that the student can correctly evaluate the content, not that they have bet on the length of the item.

Matching Items

Matching items are exercises that give students a list of premises, which are numbered as the test items, and a list of possible responses, which typically are labeled with letters. Each response is available for any premise within the exercise. For this reason, the exercise should consist of fewer than 10 premises; it is almost impossible to come up with more than 10 responses that are plausible choices for every premise on a longer list. Matching exercises typically assess recall, although some variations of matching exercises (not discussed in this chapter) can assess application.

Matching exercises should have directions that include the basis for matching. Directions that simply tell students to "match" or to write letters next to the numbers are not very helpful. Include directions for how to make their selections, for example, "Match the name of the painting with the name of the painter who created it." Many students may be able to figure out the basis for the matching, but it's not their job to do so. It is your responsibility to make clear what kind of selection you are asking students to do.

Matching exercises should be homogeneous, as in the paintings-and-painters example above. If they're not, students can use logic rather than content knowledge to select their response (e.g., "This one has to be a person's name," "This one has to be the name of a city," etc.). When they do that, the exercise tests logic, not the content of the learning goal.

When you construct a matching exercise, make the longer phrases the premises and the shorter ones the responses. When students do a matching exercise, they typically read the premises one time each and cycle through the responses many times. If the responses are the shorter of the two, students will be able to do that more easily. For a similar reason, if there is an order to the responses (e.g., chronological order for dates, alphabetical order for names), use that order for the responses. If a student knows an answer outright, if there is an order to the responses, they can just look it up instead of reading through all the responses. For example, consider a matching exercise with historical events as premises and years as responses. If the responses were ordered chronologically, a student who knew the response for the premise "Year World War 1 began" should be "1914" could locate it easily without having to read through all the dates they could select.

Finally, make sure that students cannot use the process of elimination when they get to the last matching item. That will happen if there are exactly the same number of premises and responses and if students can only use each response once. In that case, the last point in a matching exercise doesn't mean much. There are two ways to avoid this kind of "perfect matching." Either have at least one more response than there are premises or allow students to use the same response more than once. In either case, make sure your directions tell students whether responses can be used only once or more than once.

Multiple-Choice Items

Multiple-choice items consist of a stem—the question—and typically three to five choices from which students select an answer. Multiple-choice items are very common in both classroom and large-scale testing. One advantage of multiple-choice items is that they can assess recall, understanding, and application—even sometimes analysis—depending on how the item is written.

When you write a multiple-choice item, make sure the stem actually asks a question and doesn't merely bring up a topic. The stem can either be a true question, ending with a question mark, or it can be an incomplete sentence that implies a question. If the latter, the implied question should be clear and something that all students, even those who don't know the answer, could identify.

The answer choices, sometimes called options, consist of a key (the correct answer) and distractors (incorrect answers). The term "distractor" simply means that the choice is a plausible one for students who do not know the answer; it doesn't mean that the distractors should be tricky or confusing to students who do. The question should have a single correct or best answer, which is clear to students who know the content. Students who do not should find all the choices, both key and distractors, plausible alternatives.

You can get more information out of a multiple-choice item if your distractors are based on common misconceptions. In that case, students' selections give you information about concepts that need clarification or reteaching.

"All of the above" does not work as a distractor. In a four-choice item, for example, if a student knows two of the choices are correct and has no idea about a third, but the fourth choice is "all of the above," the student would choose it and get the item correct. However, that score does not mean what it is intended to mean, namely that the student understands everything in the question.

"None of the above" only works in special situations. It can, for example, work in items where students need to solve math problems. If the student solves the problem and gets an answer that is not among the options, they can choose "none of the above" if it's available. If you write this kind of item, however, "none of the above" should actually be the correct answer sometimes, so that students do not simply learn it is never correct and turn it into a nonfunctioning distractor.

The further reading resources discuss many varieties of multiple-choice items beyond the basic type discussed here. One of them, *context-dependent items*, is important enough to mention here because it is one of the key ways to create multiple-choice items that measure higher-order thinking. Context-dependent items, sometimes called interpretive exercises, present students with introductory material. That material may be in the form of text, graphs or charts, drawings, maps, or any other way to present content for students to think about. With the advent of computers, the material can also include video or audio recordings or interactive demonstrations. Then one or more questions follow, often including multiple-choice questions. You may be most familiar with this type of item from tests in reading, which often include excerpts from texts as introductory material and then ask questions about it.

Figure 15.2 shows an example of a context-dependent item set. In this item, the diagram of the electrical circuit is the introductory material. To answer the question, students need to apply what they know about conductivity. You could add to this item a space for a short answer and ask, "Explain how you chose your answer." Depending on the test plan, the resulting multiple-choice-plus-explanation item could be scored using a multiple point rubric or scoring scheme.

FIGURE 15.2
Example of a Context-Dependent Multiple-Choice Item

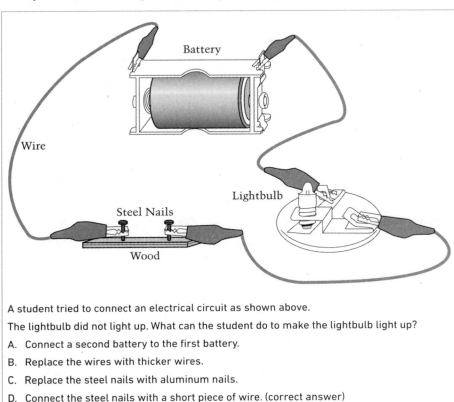

A student tried to connect an electrical circuit as shown above.

The lightbulb did not light up. What can the student do to make the lightbulb light up?

A. Connect a second battery to the first battery.

B. Replace the wires with thicker wires.

C. Replace the steel nails with aluminum nails.

D. Connect the steel nails with a short piece of wire. (correct answer)

Source: NAEP released item 2009-4S11 #13.

How Do I Involve Students in Selected Response Test Questions?

You can involve students in the writing of selected response test questions, as mentioned in Chapter 14, by having them write practice test items according to your test plan. Then, students can use the items they created in classroom review, in competitive games or collaborative group work, or in at-home studying.

You can involve students in responding to selected response test questions in several ways. Many students enjoy seeing the results of classroom response systems that graph the distribution of responses during classroom formative assessment. You can post the distribution and ask students why they think others might have selected each of the choices.

Another way to involve students in multiple-choice questions is to use one where you suspect responses will differ, and use those responses to have students group themselves (all those who chose answer A go to this corner, all those who chose answer B go to that corner, etc.). In their groups, students discuss why they chose the answer they did and whether they would change it. In the process, they deal with the content of the learning goal. A variation of this is to group students heterogeneously (e.g., a group of four students who chose answers A, B, C, and D respectively), and have them discuss among themselves until they come to a consensus on a group answer and can explain why.

What Are Some Common Misconceptions About Selected Response Test Questions?

Probably the most common misconception about selected response test questions is that they only test recall of memorized material. As this chapter showed, some selected response questions, most notably multiple choice and sometimes true-false, can test understanding and application, as well.

Another misconception is that selected response test questions, or sometimes just multiple-choice questions, mean standardized testing. Item format (multiple choice or whatever it is) is a separate issue from whether a test is standardized, that is, whether it has regulated the conditions of administration such that scores from different testing contexts can be compared (see Chapter 21 for more on standardized testing). Selected response questions can be quite useful in classroom assessment.

FOR FURTHER READING

Brookhart, S. (2014). *How to design questions and tasks to assess student thinking.* ASCD.

Brookhart, S. M., & Nitko, A. J. (2019). *Educational assessment of students* (8th ed.). Pearson.

Chappuis, J., & Stiggins, R. (2020). *Classroom assessment for student learning: Doing it right—using it well* (3rd ed.). Pearson.

16

Writing Constructed Response Test Questions

What Are Constructed Response Test Questions?

Constructed response test questions are test questions to which students respond by constructing their own answer, typically by writing, drawing, diagramming, or graphing. Constructed response test questions cover a broad range of tasks, from filling in a word or phrase in a test item to extended essays. Constructed response test questions include essay questions in any discipline and show-the-work (or show-the-work-and-explain-your-reasoning) problems on math and science tests. This chapter deals with constructed response test questions suitable for inclusion on a test. More extensive student constructions, such as extended written work or complex projects, are treated in Chapters 12 and 13.

Why Are Constructed Response Test Questions Important?

Effective constructed response questions require students to use higher-order thinking skills specified in their learning goals. Constructed response questions can often tap aspects of the domain of learning specified in a standard that are not as easily accessed with selected response items. This, in turn, is important because you want your test to be as representative as possible of the learning domain of the standard(s) you intend to assess. This chapter shows how to write essay and show-the-work questions that align to intended content and thinking skills while still producing clear, scorable work.

How Do I Use Constructed Response Test Questions in My Teaching and Assessment?

Questions can be categorized according to whether they are *closed* (have one correct answer) or *open* (have more than one possible good answer). Constructed response questions can also be categorized according to the length or form of their answers. Some constructed response questions only require a word or phrase and are essentially fill-in-the-blank questions without a word bank. More extensive constructed response questions can be *short answer* (sometimes called restricted response) or *extended response* questions.

For constructed response test questions that only require a word or phrase—that is, for fill-in-the-blank questions that do not tap higher-order thinking—use closed questions that follow the guidelines given in Chapter 15 for fill-in questions. Here are some examples.

- What is 4 times 5? (Remember)
- What is a whole number? (Understand)
- What is the next number in the series: 1, 4, 7, 10, ... (Apply)

For short-answer questions and extended-response questions, aim to use open questions that require thinking at the Analyze, Evaluate, or Create level. The reasoning behind this recommendation is that on a test, measuring thinking at the Remember, Understand, and Apply levels is more efficiently done with selected response items or fill-in items. Short answer and extended response questions often use multiple-point scoring (a rubric or scoring scheme) and typically take longer to score. You can get more student responses (more test items) with less scoring time if you use selected response questions, which are perfectly suited for the job. Use short answer or extended response questions to cover that part of the learning domain that can't be easily assessed with selected response questions—those aspects of the learning goal that require thinking at the Analyze, Evaluate, or Create levels. In addition, students need more time to answer constructed response questions that require higher-order thinking. Save that effort for aspects of the standard that selected response items do not assess well. Depending on the standard(s) you intend to assess, you may find yourself creating a test that is comprised of only selected response items, only constructed response items, or both. Very often, it will be both.

The foundation for writing short answer or extended response essay questions or show-the-work problems is the same as for writing selected response test questions. Effective short answer or extended response questions do the following:

- Elicit content and thinking skills required by the learning goal you intend to assess.
- Do not require irrelevant content and thinking skills.
- Match your test plan in terms of number and point value.

The rhetorical foundations for writing short answer or extended response questions are the same as for selected response questions, as well. Effectively written constructed response items should do the following:

- Use language that is as simple and straightforward as possible.
- Avoid wording that is identical to the textbook or other materials.
- Avoid language that gives a clue to the answer of this or another question.

In addition to these foundational principles for writing test questions, there are specific guidelines for writing short answer or extended response questions for assessing learning goals in content areas. Figure 16.1 summarizes these. Finally, both short answer and extended response test questions can employ introductory material, as do context-dependent multiple-choice items. You can present text, graphs or charts, drawings, maps, or other content for students to think about before asking the question. This has the advantage of giving all students immediate access to the material they need to think about.

Short Answer (Restricted Response) Items

Short answer items can be anything from a sentence to several paragraphs, depending on the content and grade level you are working with. In any case, they should ask one clear, focused question and call for students to give a brief, focused response. Using several short answer questions instead of one extended response question helps you cover more aspects of the learning domain and also get more samples of students' thinking. For those reasons, using several short answer questions instead of one long one is preferred unless the standard requires you to assess extended thinking.

Even if the answer is to be short, ask a question that requires higher-order thinking. Figure 16.1 lists some examples but is by no means exhaustive. The idea is that you should use constructed responses to test things

FIGURE 16.1

Guidelines for Writing Constructed Response Test Questions

Short Answer (Restricted Response) Items

- Use several short answer items instead of one extended response item unless the standard requires an extended response.
- Ask clearly for a focused response to one point.
- Ask a question that requires higher-order thinking, for example:
  » Explain cause and effect.
  » Identify assumptions or limitations.
  » Draw valid conclusions from premises.
  » State a position or opinion and support it.
  » Explain a procedure.
  » Compare and contrast ideas.
  » Solve a problem and explain reasoning.
- Use clear scoring criteria, shared with students if possible.
- Avoid optional questions.

Extended Response Items

- Use to assess deep understanding of a small range of content.
- Use open questions that require higher-order thinking.
- If the question asks a student's opinion, make clear that their answers will be assessed on the logic and evidence they use, not the position they take.
- Use wording that helps all students interpret the question in the way you intended.
- Specify expectations for both content and organization.
- Clarify the required or intended length of the answer and the suggested amount of time students should devote to it.
- Use clear scoring criteria, shared with students if possible.
- Allow enough time for thinking and writing.

that you couldn't as easily test with selected responses, because these items take longer for both students to answer and you to score.

As with any question or task that will be assessed with multi-point scoring or a rubric with performance level descriptions, share those scoring criteria with students if possible—and it should almost always be possible. In fact, the only time it shouldn't be possible is if the scoring scheme is task-specific, for example, if it says that the student's answer to the problem is 125 pounds and the explanation describes one of three specified strategies. This kind of scoring is generally not recommended for classroom tests for the very reason that it can't be shared with students. In the case of this example, a more general math problem solving rubric that students could apply to other problems would be better because it would help students learn and generalize the principles for effective math problem solving and communication. In addition, using task-specific scoring schemes means teachers have to create a new scoring scheme for every problem, which is very time-consuming.

Avoiding optional questions can sometimes seem controversial. In many aspects of instruction and assessment, giving students choices is recommended. These guidelines mean to say that for a classroom test that serves as a summative assessment, avoid optional questions. Research has shown that students do not, in fact, always select the question that shows their thinking to its best advantage. Also, different questions will have different difficulty levels, so they assess the content differently. Optional questions are very helpful for most formative assessment purposes, for instructional purposes (e.g., for use in learning stations), and for performance assessment, where the choices students make can be part of what is assessed (see Chapter 12 for more details about performance tasks).

Here is an example of a short answer question that follows these guidelines, from middle school U.S. History, adapted from NAEP Released item 2006-8H9 #4:

> At the Constitutional Convention in 1787, the large states and the small states disagreed with each other about how the new government should be structured. Identify the most important issue that large and small states disagreed about. Explain how this issue was resolved by the Connecticut (Great) Compromise. [Issues – 2 points, Explanation – 2 points]

This question can be answered in a brief paragraph. It requires students to remember and understand that the Great Compromise was the creation of a bicameral legislature, that is, a legislature with two houses. In the Senate, large and small states had equal representation; in the House of Representatives, states had representation based on their population. The question also requires students to explain what the issue was and how this solution resolved it. The quality of the student's explanation is assessed as well as their recall.

Extended Response Items

Extended response questions can be a paragraph or more for younger students and a true essay for older students. As for short answer questions, use questions that require higher-order thinking. It isn't worth the time and effort required of both students and teachers to use an extended response item to, for example, replicate an explanation of a historical event from a textbook or a list of scientific procedures. Those sorts of learning goals are much more efficiently and effectively assessed with selected response items.

The difference between an extended response essay test question and a performance assessment where a student is assigned to do an extended essay can be a fuzzy line. This chapter discusses extended response essays or extended problems to solve that would be on a test students would complete in a class period. Longer essays, while following most of the same guidelines as essay test questions, are usually considered performance assessments.

The more complex the question and the more extended the response, the more students' responses will differ—and therefore the more difficult it will be for you to assess them in a comparable manner. As for any assessment, use clear scoring criteria and share them with students. The guidelines for writing extended constructed response questions all focus on helping students interpret the question in the way you intended and construct, if not identical, at least similarly scorable answers. This is the reasoning behind the suggestions to use clear wording that all students will most likely interpret in the same way, specifying both what the question is asking and how the answer should be organized, and giving directions for length. All of these suggestions are meant to help all students form a similar conception of what is being asked and what they might do to respond. The "openness" in students' responses to open-ended questions should be demonstrations of the knowledge and thinking they bring to the content, not demonstrations of varying ways of interpreting what the question asked.

Sometimes, extended response test questions ask students to apply what they know to a controversial topic, or even a topic that is not controversial but does allow for several points of view. If you use an extended response test question that asks students to do this, make sure that first, the opinion and argument you request elicit knowledge and thinking from the learning domain you are assessing, and second, that students know they will not be evaluated based on the position they take but rather on the quality of their argument. If you draft an "opinion" question where one opinion is correct and another is not, revise the question to ask about the content in another way.

Figure 16.2 is an example of an extended response question that follows the guidelines, from middle or high school science.

How Do I Involve Students in Constructed Response Test Questions?

You can involve students in the writing of constructed response test questions, as for selected response questions, by having them write practice test

FIGURE 16.2
Example of an Extended Response Question

A small town is located on the seashore, separated from the ocean by sand. The ocean erodes the sand a little each year. The town council is trying to decide what conservation measures they could take to prevent further erosion. Name two strategies that might reduce or prevent the erosion of the sand, and explain how each strategy would work. Describe the advantages and disadvantages to the environment that each strategy would bring, and decide which strategy you would recommend to the town council based on your comparison of these advantages and disadvantages. Your answer should be at least three paragraphs and take about 15 minutes. It will be evaluated with the following rubric.

Criterion	5	3	1
Conservation methods	I name two methods that would reduce or prevent the erosion of sand and describe them completely and accurately.	I name one method that would reduce or prevent the erosion of sand and describe it accurately, or I name two methods but don't describe them accurately.	I name a method that would not reduce or prevent sand erosion, or I don't name any method.
Advantages and disadvantages of each method	I clearly explain the environmental advantages and disadvantages that would result from each conservation method.	I clearly explain the environmental advantages and disadvantages that would result from one conservation method, or I explain only advantages or disadvantages.	My explanations of environmental advantages and disadvantages of the conservation methods are not clear, or I don't explain advantages and disadvantages.
Comparison and recommendation	I make a clear recommendation and support it by a clear comparison of the environmental advantages and disadvantages of each conservation method.	I make a recommendation, but my comparison of each method is not clear.	I don't make a recommendation, or I make a recommendation that is not supported by my comparison of the methods.

items according to your test plan. Then, students can use the items they created in classroom review.

You can also use practice questions, written by students or by yourself or adapted from other materials, to help students learn how to answer questions effectively. In class or in small groups, you can discuss what makes a good answer for a given question and why. You can have students make suggestions for improvement of answers you create that are incomplete, inaccurate, or inappropriate in some way. Students should discuss the substance of the question—what would make a better answer to more fully represent understanding of the content—not just suggestions for improving the writing.

What Are Some Common Misconceptions About Constructed Response Test Questions?

As mentioned in the last chapter, there is a common misconception that constructed response questions are good and selected response questions are bad, probably because many standardized tests use selected response items. In fact, this is not true. Constructed response questions are best for tapping into student thinking and application of content, but they are not typically the most effective way to find out about student knowledge of facts.

For example, "List and define the four states of matter" is not a good use of a constructed response question. A set of selected response questions would yield a better estimate of student understanding of the states of matter. This question would elicit memorized information that may not receive full marks for irrelevant reasons (e.g., a student misspelled a term, or left out a term they knew, or wrote a poor explanation because of poor writing skills). Further, just being able to reproduce a list of terms and definitions does not necessarily mean that the student understands them. Finally, this question would require more student testing time and teacher scoring time than a set of selected response items that would produce a more valid measure of the same knowledge.

The key is to use constructed response test questions when the learning about which you need evidence requires that students actually construct, not just select, an answer. Such learning goals are, as the chapter has shown, typically about students' abilities to analyze or evaluate material, create new material, or solve problems and explain their thinking.

FOR FURTHER READING

Brookhart, S. (2014). *How to design questions and tasks to assess student thinking.* ASCD.

Brookhart, S. M., & Nitko, A. J. (2019). *Educational assessment of students* (8th ed.). Pearson.

Chappuis, J., & Stiggins, R. (2020). *Classroom assessment for student learning: Doing it right—using it well* (3rd ed.). Pearson.

17

Using Portfolio Assessment

What Is Portfolio Assessment?

Portfolios are purposeful collections of student work that include student reflections on the work. They are intended to present evidence for one of two purposes: to showcase the student's best work or to demonstrate growth over time. The construction of these two types of portfolios is different. For a best-work portfolio, students and teachers select work that illustrates a student's attainment of learning goals, and the student reflections or annotations typically describe what the work—collectively or piece-by-piece, depending on the portfolio design—shows the student knows and can do. For a growth portfolio, students and teachers select work that illustrates a student's growth or development over time; for example, a writing growth portfolio might contain pieces written at the beginning, middle, and end of the year, including initial drafts, revisions, and final work for each. The student annotations or reflections would typically describe how the pieces viewed in sequence represent what and how they learned. The intentionality and the student reflection distinguish portfolios from other collections of students' work, such as the weekly folders (paper or digital) some elementary teachers send home that contain all the student's work for the week. Figure 17.1 shows some general examples of each type of portfolio.

Why Is Portfolio Assessment Important?

Portfolios are an important assessment option because they exhibit the evidence—the student work—upon which conclusions about student learning

FIGURE 17.1
Examples of Portfolio Purposes and Content

Purpose	Examples
Best-work portfolio: To showcase student achievement or accomplishment in an area	• A portfolio of evidence to show mastery of subject-matter learning for one or more standards, for formative classroom assessment and possibly grading, or sharing with parents/guardians. Student work and reflections are organized by standard and evaluated with a rubric. • A portfolio of evidence of exceptional achievement in an area, especially in a creative area such as writing or the arts, for demonstrating high-level accomplishment for admissions (e.g., to art school), placement, or awards (e.g., a merit badge or school award). • A portfolio of evidence of basic competence in a subject as part of a qualification (e.g., for graduation). Student work and reflections are organized by graduation (or other) requirements.
Growth portfolio: To showcase student growth or development in an area	• A portfolio of evidence of progress in areas that develop over time (e.g., writing, problem solving, communications). Student work and reflections are typically organized in chronological order. Reflections explain how each subsequent entry shows student development and improvement.

are drawn and decisions about future learning are made. Viewing a collection of evidence allows students themselves, their parents or guardians, and their teachers to get a richer picture of learning than, for example, a test score can give. Portfolios show what students' achievement looks like.

From the late 1980s to mid-1990s, several states experimented with using portfolio assessment for large-scale state accountability assessment. In general, research on those efforts led to the conclusion that large-scale portfolio use was too unreliable and too expensive to serve state accountability purposes well. Research on unstandardized portfolio use for purposes of classroom learning has been much more sanguine. Portfolios are particularly suited to assessing the writing process and other creative processes (e.g., visual arts). Portfolios can also be effective for formative assessment of classroom learning goals in many other subjects. Research has shown that portfolios are most effective for formative purposes, although they can be graded in certain circumstances.

How Do I Use Portfolio Assessment in My Teaching and Assessment?

You can think about planning for portfolio use in terms of four steps. First, Identify the purpose and focus for the portfolio. Second, decide what entries the portfolio will include and how they will be organized. Third, plan the practical and logistical aspects of portfolio use, including whether and how you will leverage technology to make the logistics manageable. Finally, evaluate the portfolios and the effectiveness of the portfolio experience.

Identify the Portfolio's Purpose

Why do you want to use a portfolio? This question often can be answered by filling in two blanks: *I want to use a portfolio of evidence of student learning of [statement of the standard(s) or learning goal(s) the portfolio will address] in order to [statement about how you and students will use the evidence].* This first step may be the last, because sometimes in identifying the portfolio's purpose a teacher will realize the same purpose could be better served with a performance assessment or a test.

Once you are convinced that a portfolio is an appropriate approach, think about the implications of your purpose statement. Does your purpose imply a best-works portfolio or a growth and progress portfolio? Is the major use formative (primarily to support learning, not graded) or summative (primarily to evaluate learning, graded)? What aspects of the portfolio will be emphasized? In a portfolio whose purpose is formative, the quality of the work and the quality of students' reflections and formative use of the portfolio are emphasized more or less equally. In a portfolio whose purpose is summative, the quality of the final work is emphasized more. How will students be involved in portfolio construction and use? Should parents be involved (e.g., will the portfolio form the basis for a student-parent conference)? Should the portfolio be paper or digital?

Decide on Portfolio Entries and Organization

It is important to decide what will go in the portfolio and what will not. Overstuffed or unorganized portfolios cannot provide useful evidence of learning. Portfolios consist of two general types of entries or files: student work products and students' reflections on that work. They often have a table of contents that also serves as an organizing framework.

The two most common organizing frameworks are categories based on the content of the learning standard(s) or chronological order. The organizing framework should match the purpose of the portfolio. For example, in a best-works portfolio for a 5th grade math class that is specifically targeted to learning standards about fractions, the work might be organized into categories: adding and subtracting fractions; multiplying and dividing fractions; using fractions to model and solve word problems. Students might select each piece for its ability to demonstrate something about their learning in one of those categories and explain their choice on a sticky note or digital tag. For another example, a portfolio intended to show 4th grade students' growth and development in writing over a year might be organized chronologically by month. Within each month, a plan, draft, revision, and edited version of the same piece might be accompanied by student reflections, and an overall reflection of progress across the year in producing clear and coherent writing with attention to task, purpose, and audience might be the final entry. Although categories and chronology are common, other organizing frameworks may be used. The key is that the portfolio organizes the student work and reflections into evidence that matches the purpose of the portfolio.

However organized, as for all assessment, the student work should represent the domain of learning the portfolio is meant to address. Also, for each piece of work, whether intended as formative or summative assessment, the criteria by which students and teachers can discern the quality of the work, its current strengths and weaknesses, and next steps should be available. Reflection on work without criteria is baseless. Individual pieces may have individual rubrics or any one of the many other ways of communicating criteria. Sometimes the whole portfolio has an overall rubric, as well, that centers on how the set of exhibits of student work and reflections in the portfolio informs its purpose. Sometimes those are common, schoolwide rubrics (Niguidula, 2019). Sometimes each piece uses the same rubric as, for example, a writing portfolio may look at all pieces through the lens of a general writing rubric.

Decisions about portfolio entries and organization should, in the end, be specific enough to support plans for classroom implementation. It's not enough to say, for example, "Writing will be collected over time." More useful would be to say, "One narrative, persuasive, or expository piece per month will be collected, in complete form including plan, first draft, revision, and final edited copy. Students, in consultation with the teacher, may choose which piece they enter each month."

You also should specify whether the portfolio entries will be assessed individually before they go in the portfolio. Typically they are, but not necessarily. It depends on the purpose of the portfolio.

Finally, decide on the nature of the student reflections or annotations that will go in the portfolio. Many options exist. For some work, a sticky note of explanation or a digital tag will suffice. Sometimes, teachers design reflection forms (paper or electronic, depending on the portfolio design) to go with portfolio entries, for individual pieces or groups of entries.

Sometimes, students write essay-style reflections; these can be based on the criteria for the assignments or on open-ended questions teachers pose, but they should be based on something to avoid unhelpful reflections such as "I liked this story."

Plan the Practical and Logistical Aspects of Portfolio Use

Once you know what the portfolio should contain and how it should be organized, you need plans for sharing this information with students and plans for how it will happen during class time. For example, students might work on their portfolios for 15 minutes every Thursday or for 10 minutes at the beginning of class every day during a unit (for constructing a unit-related portfolio). For some kinds of portfolios, time for students sharing portfolios with partners or student-teacher conferences about the portfolios might be planned. In addition to such logistics, students should be taught what "working on the portfolio" means. They need to know, for example, what work should be selected and by whom (student, teacher, or both), how they should do their reflections, if and when the portfolio will be evaluated or graded (if that is part of the purpose), and so on. Students should know how to connect the reflections they do on their work in the portfolio with ongoing classroom work.

Students also need to know the logistics of the exercise. For example, if the portfolios are in folders kept in crates in the room, how do students retrieve them and refile them? Are they allowed to work on them any time or just during designated portfolio time? If the folders are digital, the questions are similar, but the directions will be different: Where are the files stored and when and how are students allowed to access them? If there is portfolio software, how do students learn to use it?

Finally, one of the primary purposes of using portfolios as opposed to other forms of assessment is that the portfolio showcases both the evidence (the student work) as well as the results (grades, scores, feedback, etc.) and also student reflection on their work, which helps students with the regulation of learning. You wouldn't do all that unless you were going to use those elements to help students process what they were learning, helping them see how they are learning and developing metacognitive and self-regulatory skills and self-efficacy for learning that content. Therefore, plans for portfolio use should include how you will connect "portfolio time" with students' ongoing learning. This is an issue both for lesson planning and for planning the questions you will use as you discuss students' learning with them. I have, for example, observed elementary school teachers having students write about their reading and share their latest portfolio entry in small groups; this led to productive discussions about both writing quality and the content of the texts they read.

Evaluate the Portfolios and the Effectiveness of the Portfolio Experience

Best-works portfolios often contain work that has been evaluated at the time the students did it (e.g., a set of science problems, with work shown and reasoning explained and teacher feedback or a score or grade on it, may be included in the portfolio). Growth portfolios may include some drafts of work that do not receive a score or grade, but have feedback from teacher, peers, or student self-reflection. Students should know what will happen with those evaluations. What will you learn from them, and how will you use them? If the portfolio is formative in nature, your plans for connecting portfolio evidence to further learning, discussed in the previous section, is the main answer to this question. If the portfolio is summative in nature, you should have plans for how you will grade. For example, if you grade each piece students should know how each piece is weighted in the final grade. Or if you are using the most recent work to represent student proficiency on a single standard, students should know how you will evaluate that.

In addition to evaluating the portfolios and making sure they do fulfill their purpose—a portfolio languishing on a shelf or in a computer file never helped anyone—it is a good idea to evaluate the portfolio experience. The purpose of portfolios, in general, is to emphasize evidence as much as results. What did the presence of all this evidence add to your teaching and to student learning? Was the evidence you and the students received from the portfolio work worth the time and effort it took to collect and use it? What did students learn from keeping the portfolio, doing their reflections, and applying them to their work? What did you learn from observing that work and from the in-process and finished portfolios? What changes would you make to your portfolio plans the next time you decide to use a portfolio? The answers to many of these questions will depend on the context of your own classroom, your students, and their learning.

How Do I Involve Students in Portfolio Assessment?

By definition, portfolios are learner-centered. Students collect evidence of their learning and reflect on its meaning. Portfolios show students what they are learning and what they have learned. The amount of student involvement in the selection of portfolio entries will vary with grade level and content. Always aim for maximum possible student involvement, so that portfolios become the students' record, not yours.

In addition, students are always involved in reflection on their work. Student reflection is what distinguishes a portfolio from other collections of student work, like weekly take-home folders. As for the development of any skill, teach students how to do thoughtful, effective reflections, which don't come naturally. Teach reflection as you would teach anything: help students understand the criteria for a thoughtful reflection, model doing reflection, have students practice reflection, and give feedback. The results will be well worth it. Surface-level reflections such as "It was a fun project" are not very helpful, but thoughtful student reflection against criteria that represent what they are trying to learn is a powerful booster for learning.

Finally, portfolio use seems to, more than other assessment methods, collect stories about students and their work, probably because the method is so learner-centered. Examples abound, but one will suffice here to illustrate the power of story to inspire portfolio use. Hebert (2001) tells the story of Tim, one of four 2nd graders who had been invited to a 1st grade class in May to help the 1st graders prepare for their portfolio conferences with their parents. In an effort to show the 1st graders what his portfolio showed him, he held out two pieces of writing, one from his 1st grade writing journal and one from his 2nd grade portfolio. He said to the 1st graders, "See?" His teacher realized what was about to happen and asked him what he wanted the 1st graders to see.

> "Well," he said, "there are more words on this page. I use upper and lower case letters here." And as if just then realizing the difference between his 1st grade and 2nd grade writing he simply added, thrusting one fist forward and then the other for emphasis, "This is words; but *this* is a story." (Hebert, 2001, p. 2)

What Are Some Common Misconceptions About Portfolio Assessment?

Perhaps not a true misconception, but more of a conundrum, is the ongoing discussion about what a portfolio actually is. Some describe portfolio assessment as an assessment method, and it is certainly used that way in many classrooms. Others see portfolios as a method of communicating about assessment, in that sense in the same category as report card grades, student-parent conferences, or narrative reports. Others see portfolios blurring the line between assessment and instruction. An effective portfolio is as much a tool for learning, as the student constructs and reviews it and makes decisions about next steps, as it is an assessment. This chapter has shown that a portfolio is a little bit of all three of these, and perhaps best described as the research has shown: the best use of a portfolio is to support formative assessment and student self-reflection. In other words, portfolios do blur the line between assessment and instruction, as does all effective formative assessment, and they do help communicate information about learning. Although this may seem a bit of a conundrum, the fact that portfolios exist in this intersection is the source of their effectiveness.

FOR FURTHER READING

Hebert, E. A. (2001). *The power of portfolios: What children can teach us about learning and assessment.* Jossey-Bass.

Niguidula, D. (2019). *Demonstrating student mastery with digital badges and portfolios.* ASCD.

Renwick, M. (2014). *Digital student portfolios: A whole school approach to connected learning and continuous assessment.* Powerful Learning Press.

18

Grading and Reporting on Student Learning

What Is Grading?

The main purpose of grading and reporting on student learning is to communicate with students, parents, and others about the status of a student's learning on a specific standard or subject at the time the grade is given. There are many ways to assign grades on individual pieces of student work and many ways to aggregate them into one summary grade for a report card. Some of those ways serve communication purposes better than others, and some support student learning better than others. Grading also serves as a kind of feedback sometimes called "knowledge of results" by educational psychologists.

Knowing the results of an assessment gives students some information about their learning, but grades are by nature a summary measure. One score, mark, or grade summarizes achievement. Extended feedback, such as comments based on criteria or analyses of strengths and areas for improvement, gives students more actionable information. Therefore, this chapter describes ways to use grades to report student learning and recommends more extended feedback (see Chapter 4) instead of grades to provide students with formative feedback for next steps. In other words, this chapter treats grades as summative measures.

Why Is Grading Important?

Grading is perhaps the most common educational measure. Students and parents expect grades to answer the question "How am I (or how is my child) doing?" The main reason grades should indicate students' current achievement status on a standard or subject (depending on how the report card is structured) is because parents, students, and others make decisions as if this were the case. For example, teachers make decisions about students' placement based in part on their grades. Students make decisions about future careers or areas of study based on grades. Therefore, it is important that the academic grade carry meaning about learning, as untainted as possible with information about other things that can creep into grades: behavior (e.g., attendance, late work, bringing supplies to class), attitudes, work habits, classroom citizenship, and so on. Those other things can be assessed by classroom observation and sometimes checklists, given feedback and rewarded or coached for improvement, but should not be graded. They can be indicated separately on a report card, as well. The key is to make sure the academic grade accurately represents students' status in a learning domain, and behavior and work habits are accurately represented separately, so that sound information and good decisions result.

To further this argument, consider that the use of grades is woven into the fabric of schooling and into students' and teachers' discourse about learning. Grades also serve some of the administrative functions that come with doing education at scale, for example, aggregating information for evaluating programs or evaluating students for placement decisions. To serve any of these purposes well, grades need to be measures of student achievement of intended learning outcomes (typically, standards, but whatever learning goals are the basis for instruction).

If academic grades are to indicate learning, it follows that what is graded—the assessments and assignments to which a grade is assigned—must be valid measures of student learning. This is the reason tests and performance assessments need plans in place to link them to learning outcomes, and why questions and tasks should be carefully crafted to elicit evidence of specific student learning (see Chapters 12 to 17). No amount of effective grading practices can pull valid information from invalid assessments.

How Do I Use Grading in My Teaching and Assessment?

Grades from individual summative assessments—those assessments intended to summarize student learning after learning has occurred, that is, not formative assessment—are typically collected into a gradebook and then summarized into a final grade for a standard or subject area, depending on how the report card is structured. You can practice learning-focused grading whether your school uses standards-based grading or traditional grading. To do this, make sure grades represent the learning domain for the intended learning outcome(s) at two levels:

- Does the individual assignment elicit, and does the grade encode, evidence of the learning it is intended to report?
- Does the composite grade encode evidence of the learning it is intended to report?

Grading Individual Assessments

First, make sure you select the assessments that you will grade with the learning goals in mind. Design tests and performance assessments with strategies that ensure the questions and tasks, as well as the scoring schemes you will use to grade them, map directly onto the learning goal(s), and that in all other ways these assessments are of high quality. Also make sure that students have had enough time with formative work—starting with understanding the learning targets and criteria, doing formative practice work, receiving feedback, and doing self-reflection—that the appropriate time has come to take a grade. Make sure daily lessons match the learning goals as well, that students have had appropriate differentiation of instruction based on their formative work. Without all of that in place, summative (graded) assessments cannot yield valid information.

Second, inform students about upcoming graded assessments so they have time to study and prepare. Pop quizzes, a strategy from yesteryear, is and always has been more about controlling behavior than indicating learning. If an assessment is to indicate students' current best work, they need time to prepare. Give the students all the information they need (e.g., when a test will be given or a project due, how much time they should spend on it, how you will grade it, what it's supposed to show about their learning) to prepare wisely. Give them scaffolding as needed to help them prepare. For example, you can share your test plan and have students write review questions to match it. You can give students time to share projects and receive feedback.

Third, grade achievement, and handle behavioral issues and issues about following directions separately. For example, the rubrics you use to grade an essay or project should be directly related to what the student was supposed to be learning and reflect the quality of students' learning as shown in the work. So, for example, you might assess whether students' term papers used relevant, credible sources—not whether they used three sources. Chapter 13 provides more detail on how to make criteria and performance level descriptions match learning goals.

Criteria for surface-level aspects of the work (e.g., neatness) or for following directions (e.g., used double-spacing) that are not part of the stated learning goal can be assessed with a checklist. Students can assess their own work before turning it in, or partners can check each other's work to see if directions have been followed and the work is ready to turn in. To be clear, it is not that these aspects of student work are unimportant, just that they should be kept separate from assessment of students' achievement of learning goals.

Finally, assess the learning of individuals. Grades are assigned to individuals, so the measure must fit the purpose. This is pedagogically sound, as well. True cooperative learning—the kind research has shown to improve achievement—involves group learning and individual accountability. To the extent possible, design group work that follows the cooperative learning model, where students learn together in a group and then are assessed individually. Whenever possible, redesign "group work" that amounts to having several people do one thing. This is the kind of group learning that has been shown to be fraught with difficulties, including "free riders" who rely on the work of others. If there is good reason to design a group project that has a group outcome, for example a class presentation, use the group outcome for formative feedback to the group; for grading, design some ways to uncover students' individual learning, as well, for example by using an individual follow-up test, essay or other individual written product, data display or other construction, or by requiring individual parts in the group outcome. Chapter 12 gives an example of how to do this.

Assigning Report Card Grades

Whether your school uses standards-based or traditional report cards, make sure you enter measures of achievement into your gradebook. Record and report measures of nonachievement qualities like work habits, attendance, collaboration skills, and so on separately. Organize the gradebook according to standards if you are using a standards-based report card, or by subject if you are using a traditional report card. For each standard, use a variety of different measures (e.g., a test, a performance assessment, an essay) so that the body of work as a whole represents the domain well.

When you record achievement grades in your gradebook, use the scale you will use on the report card unless there is a compelling reason not to.

This will make the grades easier to aggregate. Most report cards use either a proficiency scale (e.g., Advanced, Proficient, Nearing Proficiency, Beginning), letters (e.g., *A, B, C, D, F*), or percentages (0–100). Scales that are so disparate need to be transformed for aggregating anyway, so it's easier if you do that before you record them. If you are recording grades on a percentage scale, do not use zeros for missing work. Instead, deploy strategies to help the student finish the missing work. If that is not possible after every effort, consider using a 50–100 scale instead of a 0–100 scale so failing scores do not disproportionately affect the mean. Guskey (2020) gives a more detailed rationale for this recommendation.

When you transform grades, you do not necessarily need to use the same cut score for each assessment. Many teachers are familiar with grading policies that state, for example, 90–100 percent = *A*, 80–89 percent = *B*, and so on. Judgments of proficiency should be made on the basis of what students were asked to do and how well they did it. For performance assessment and for some essay test questions, rubrics handle this with performance level descriptions for each proficiency level, and the work is matched to the descriptions. So, for example, if an essay displays the characteristics listed for a Proficient essay, then the grade is Proficient. For selected response tests, different cut scores or logic rules may apply. A student may be deemed Proficient on one test if they get 80 percent correct on the questions dealing with a certain standard, but on another, more difficult test, Proficiency may begin at 70 percent. Whatever the grading scheme, students should be made aware of it before they take the assessment, and the decision rules should make a strong correspondence between the test content and the learning standard it is intended to assess. One exception is if *all* of your grades are on the same scale to begin with (e.g., percentages) and you need to report on another scale (e.g., letters); in that case, record the percentages and determine the letter after aggregating.

When you have collected the set of graded evidence that you will use, apply a method to determine the final grade that supports the purpose for your grade. If you are doing standards-based grading and need to report students' current achievement for each standard, weight the most recent evidence more heavily in your decision making. If you are doing traditional grading—still only considering achievement in the grade—consider the whole set of individual grades and weight the most important evidence more heavily.

Figure 18.1 describes some of the more common methods of putting individual grades together to arrive at a report card grade. The key is to select the method that returns a grade that most closely matches your purpose for

FIGURE 18.1
Common Methods for Combining Individual Grades for Reporting

Method	Type of grade and grading context	Convert individual grades to the same scale first, then follow these directions:
Recent evidence	Standards-based proficiency levels SBG	Review graded assessments within one standard in chronological order. Look for a learning curve pattern and consider the grades after the pattern levels off. Use that level (or the median, if that level fluctuates) as the grade.
Logic rule	Typically, standards-based proficiency levels; may also be used for traditional letter grading SBG, TG	Draw up a set of rules, typically in a chart, that describe a logical way to summarize achievement into each proficiency level category. For example, a student's grade on a standard will be Proficient if three out of four major assessments are Proficient or better and the remaining major and minor assessments are at least Nearing Proficient.
Median	Proficiency levels or letter grades SBG, TG	Weight individual grades, for example, by counting important assessment grades twice and then taking the median.
Mean	Numerical scales, especially percentages TG, sometimes SBG	Weight individual grades, for example, by counting important assessment grades twice and then taking the mean. If the resulting weighted mean is on the percentage scale, cut scores may be used to convert the result to *ABCDF* or some other categorical scale.

Note:
SBG = Standards-based grading
TG = Traditional grading

giving the grade. In standards-based grading, that will be reporting a student's current achievement on each standard that is graded. In traditional grading, that will usually be reporting a student's achievement summarized over all the learning goals that were taught in that class for a report period.

How Do I Involve Students in Grading?

A benefit of grading practices that report students' current status on learning goals is that involving students in grading also involves them in learning. Contrast this with grading practices that report students' earning of a mixed bag of points, where involving students usually means involving them in behaviors like bringing in supplies for extra points.

Probably the most important way to involve students in grading is to begin before that, with the formative learning cycle. In your language and in your actions, communicate to students that grades are the end result of learning that begins with clear understanding of daily learning targets and longer-term learning goals. Grades are connected to the formative practice work students do during learning because that practice work ultimately leads to the assessments that will be graded. The more students regulate their own learning during the formative learning cycle, the more they will be involved in the final outcome, their grades.

Your feedback on students' formative practice work can support student self-regulation of learning if it is tied to the criteria students are using as they learn and that you will ultimately use when you grade. This connection between formative and summative assessment via criteria also helps students understand what their grades mean: they mean the status of students' work relative to those criteria.

Students may also be involved by providing input on classroom grading policies and practices that are under your control. Examples include the logistics around how to request makeup work or retakes and redo's, what evidence students need to present when they ask, and when these things may happen. To be clear, the teacher is responsible for these policies, but discussions about what students would perceive as fair and why can go a long way to support student cooperation with you and support of each other.

What Are Some Common Misconceptions About Grading?

Two misconceptions about grades are really two sides of the same coin. Some teachers say, "If I don't grade it, they won't do it." And many teachers feel that grades are the currency that students "earn" for the work they do. Both of these sentiments imply grading practices that reward student work rather than measure student learning.

In classrooms where the culture is one of evaluation—where students are mainly working to get recognition, good grades, and other scarce resources—it may well be true that if you don't grade something, students won't do it. If you feel this is really true in your classroom, the best thing to do is work on the classroom learning climate. Changing grading practices may be part of that, but other things, especially the language you use to talk about learning and some of your classroom routines and directions, also need to change. As long as students are primarily working for grades or points rather than learning, it will be difficult to connect practice work to grading. Another way to say that is that students need to appreciate the connection between practice and their ultimate grades before they will benefit from practice or receive accurate grades.

The currency or "earning" metaphor has a long history in grading. It's easy to see how this comes from a concept of grades as reflections of what students do—including things like attendance and behavior in grades— rather than what they learn. In fact, one common way to combat this is to use a rhyme with students: Your grade is about what you *learn*, not what you *earn*. Then, of course, you need to follow this rhetoric with grading policies and practices that make it true, so students will believe it and act accordingly.

FOR FURTHER READING

Brookhart, S. M. (2017). *How to use grading to improve learning.* ASCD.

Dueck, M. (2021). *Giving students a say: Smarter assessment practices to empower and engage.* ASCD.

Feldman, J. (2019). *Grading for equity: What it is, why it matters, and how it can transform schools and classrooms.* Corwin.

Guskey, T. R. (2020). *Get set, go! Creating successful grading and reporting systems.* Solution Tree.

Guskey, T. R., & Brookhart, S. M. (Eds.). (2019). *What we know about grading: What works, what doesn't, and what's next.* ASCD.

O'Connor, K. (2022). *A repair kit for grading* (3rd ed.). First Educational Resources.

Townsley, M., & Wear, N. L. (2020). *Making grades matter: Standards-based grading in a secondary PLC at work.* Solution Tree.

19

Communicating with Parents and Guardians About Assessment

What Is Communicating About Assessment?

Other methods than grades can be used to communicate with parents and guardians about assessment. These include narrative reports, letters or emails to parents, parent-teacher conferences, and student-parent-teacher conferences. Each one of these methods is based on the same evidentiary process: set purpose, plan logistics, collect evidence, interpret evidence, and communicate.

This chapter is about communicating with parents about classroom-based assessment of learning. Parents also may need help interpreting the results of standardized tests, and this is discussed in Chapter 21.

Why Is Communicating About Assessment Important?

Most parents or guardians are interested in how their child is doing in school, for various reasons. At minimum, part of raising a child involves see-ing that they get an education. Many parents are also genuinely interested in their child's experience of school and interested in finding out where their child is doing well and where they need a little help. The time between report cards can be too long to wait for this kind of news. In addition, com-municating with parents and guardians about their child's learning is a good way to strengthen school-community relations.

The advent of parent portals and the ability to check students' grades in between report cards also brings a new reason for communicating about student learning. Looking at a list of grades from a report period yet in progress, especially those that are only summarized as a running average, may not communicate an accurate message about student learning. Parents and guardians may need guidance to help them interpret the evidence in open gradebooks.

How Do I Communicate About Assessment in My Teaching?

The processes for communicating about assessment in narrative reports, letters or emails, parent conferences, and student-parent conferences are all related—and they are also related to the processes for using portfolios to communicate about student learning (Chapter 17) and assigning grades (Chapter 18). What they all have in common is that they should be evidentiary processes: processes that start by setting a purpose; then seeking, organizing, and interpreting information to serve that purpose; and finally communicating the results. Figure 19.1 summarizes these processes. They are discussed in two sections below about narrative reports or letters (written communication) and parent-teacher or student-parent-teacher conferences (oral communication).

Written Communications About Student Work

Narrative communications are written descriptions about student work that interpret student work and sometimes provide goals for future learning. Written communication about student learning ranges on a continuum from very prescribed (e.g., selecting from a menu of comments on a report card or providing a brief sentence or phrase on a report card) to very open (e.g., using narrative report cards or sending home detailed letters or emails as needed). Writing narrative communication takes skill. Teachers must observe and synthesize a student's work and summarize those observations in a carefully crafted written text in order for the information to be clear and helpful to students and parents.

For these reasons, Power and Chandler (1998) suggest that if you want to begin writing more narrative communication, you start with one subject (for elementary) or one class (for secondary) in a report period. Begin planning how you will collect evidence by reviewing your learning goals or standards for the report period.

FIGURE 19.1
Communicating About Assessment and Learning

Process	Written narratives, letters, or email	Parent-teacher conferences	Student-parent-(teacher) conferences
Set purpose	• Progress (growth) or status (current achievement)? • What subject(s) and/or standard(s)? • Academics only or work habits as well?		Same, plus • Role of student? • Goal(s) for student participation? • Will teacher attend or not?
Gather evidence	• Student work samples • Student reflections • Observational notes		• Student work samples • Student reflections
Interpret evidence	• Draw conclusions (address the purpose) from evidence • Support and illustrate conclusions with evidence		• Help students draw conclusions • Help students decide on how to use their work to showcase their learning
Communicate results	• Written communication	• Oral communication and dialogue	• Help students practice oral presentation
Attend to response	• Require response? • Follow-up needed (e.g., schedule conference)?	• Listen to parents • Learn more about the student • Follow-up needed (e.g., strategies for class or home)?	• Celebrate student achievement • Thank parents for coming

Two or three weeks before you want to send a narrative communication, begin doing systematic observations about the students' work on the standard(s) you want to discuss. Also make sure you have some mechanism in place to collect or file the relevant student products (tests, writing, and other performance assessments). A class roster will help ensure you observe everyone.

Then, interpret those observations. Think about how you would describe the student's work, for example, how would you finish a sentence like, "Arnold's best work is in ____." Use your observations of students' work to support your conclusion. As you draft your narrative comments, make sure your conclusions are clear and connections with supporting evidence are explicit. Keep your descriptions positive, talking in terms of strengths first. When you describe challenges, make sure to suggest ways for students to meet those challenges that are realistic for the student. You can suggest both classroom follow-up and home activities. Some teachers find it is best to write the easy narratives first, building the writing skills you will need to tackle more difficult narratives.

If the narrative is on a report card, there is probably a protocol for how parents are supposed to respond. If the narrative is a letter or email to parents that is not part of the report card, specify how you would like the parent or guardian to respond. Should they email back and acknowledge they have received it? Can they request a conference if they have questions? Make it clear that you expect a response, and then follow up on the responses when they arrive.

Oral Communications About Student Work

Parent-teacher conferences, common in elementary school and less common in high school, follow a similar process as for narrative communication, except that instead of writing you must prepare to speak orally. That means you need to know the main points you want parents to hear about their child and what evidence supports them. As a new teacher many years ago, I wasn't aware of this, and I approached my middle school parent conferences armed simply with the gradebook and the intent to go over the grades with parents. Needless to say, those conferences were a huge missed opportunity. It was great to meet some of the parents and guardians, and I think they enjoyed meeting me, but I can't say that any of us left the conference with much usable information. Parents of children with high grades probably left generally feeling good, and parents of children with low grades probably left intending to ask their child to work harder, or something like that—nothing they didn't already know.

When you approach a parent conference, just as for narratives, decide on the purpose of the conference, at least from your point of view (some parents will, of course, have their own agendas). Decide what you want to be able to say about the student's learning, and whether you also want to discuss nonacademic factors like work habits or attendance. Then, collect student work samples and reflections and make your own observational notes. Draw conclusions—decide what main points you want to make—and be able to explain how your evidence supports them. If you're like me, a few notes will help keep you organized when you speak with parents.

A major difference between narratives and conferences is that in conferences, you can have a conversation with the parents or guardians. Therefore, you might want to prepare some questions that will help you understand the student and their work, for example: What kinds of things do they like to do for fun? Do they have chores or responsibilities at home, and if so how do they handle them? What kinds of things do they say about school when asked? Listen to the answers, knowing that in most cases you are talking with the people who know more about that child than anyone else in the world, including you. Together, you may be able to identify better next steps for the student than either of you acting alone. If follow-up strategies are required for academics or behavior and work habits, you have the opportunity to discuss these. What things need to happen next in school or at home to reach those next-step goals?

Parent conferences may be difficult to schedule, especially in high school. Some schools have developed strategies to make parent conferences more accessible (McKibben, 2016). For example, calling them "progress conferences" instead of "parent conferences" honors the work of all who are raising children, not just parents but guardians and foster parents as well. Setting up a space where younger siblings can come and play during the conference can help alleviate childcare issues that may be barriers to attendance for some parents.

Parents should leave the conference knowing what they have learned about their child's work in school and what you and they are going to do next. You, the teacher, should leave the conference with greater understanding of the student's background, motivation, and interests.

How Do I Involve Students in Communicating About Assessment?

Student-parent conferences place students in a leading role. The main purpose served is communicating about student learning, but done well, student-parent conferences also support student self-assessment and reflection, student ownership of learning and agency, and student and parent engagement. Student-led conferences can become part of a cultural change, where students feel in charge of their own learning and understand what and how they are progressing (Berger, 2014).

The process follows the same steps as other communication methods (see Figure 19.1). The students are responsible for describing their work, including strengths and challenges, and for setting goals. The teacher is responsible for preparing students to do this and structuring the practice they will need to do it well. Effective student-led conferences have a clear agenda and are based on a clear portfolio of work students will share. Effective practice sessions develop student self-reflection skills and presentation skills, so students can clearly communicate their learning goals and explain how their work demonstrates meeting those goals.

First, decide on the purpose of the student-parent conference. Is it to help students showcase their best works over a whole report period? Is it to share a representative sample of all the work they've been doing or to focus on a particular kind of work? The student will lead the conference, but will they also be the one to select the work to share or will you (the teacher) do that—or will you do it together?

Finally, will the teacher attend, making it a student-parent-teacher conference, or will students and parents meet alone? If the teacher does not have to attend each conference, many conferences can occur simultaneously, with the teacher present in the room but not at any one conference. For many of the purposes of student-parent conferences, the teacher's presence is not necessary and may even serve to usurp some of the student's leadership role, as parents may turn to the teacher with questions instead of to the student.

As for other communications, once you have set a purpose, decide on the student work samples and student reflections that will be shared at the conference. Student reflections are particularly important for student-parent conferences because the students will need to explain to their parents what each piece of work shows. The set of work becomes a portfolio of sorts, and the communication purpose dictates that the pieces selected not only be students' best work but also clear examples of the learning goal they are meant to illustrate, so that it is clear to the parents what they are looking at.

Sometimes, the student "work" to be collected involves a demonstration on the spot. For example, I have seen conferences in the primary grades where students demonstrated that they could count to 100, or do 20 jumping jacks, or write their letters by doing those things as part of the conference, as opposed to, for example, showing a paper where they had already written their letters.

Student-parent conferences, even those for older students, then require a planning-and-preparation phase during class. Students need to review their portfolio of work and reflect on it, typically using prompts (e.g., "What does this work show I can do with fractions?" "What does this work show about my writing?" "Which of these pieces is my favorite and why?"). Then they need to plan a presentation, similar to the way they would plan a class presentation, and practice it. What will they show first? What will they say about it? Class time devoted to getting students comfortable explaining their learning is class time well spent. It can help consolidate learning, help students practice using academic language, and help develop student self-efficacy.

Often, students write or draw invitations for their parents to invite them to student-parent conferences. Timing and other logistics can be tricky, as many parents balance crowded work and personal schedules, but if those details can be worked out, the experience can be a very positive one for both students and parents.

What Are Some Common Misconceptions Regarding Communicating About Assessment?

One common misconception is that narrative reports are always good or are somehow better than report cards. Indeed, as this chapter has shown, effective narrative reporting is difficult to do well and takes time. Ineffective narrative reporting (e.g., "Sally is a wonderful student and a delight to have in class") is not worth your time. Take the time to do narrative reporting when you have something specific to say, and when the details in the narrative report would provide useful and needed information.

Another misconception some may have is that some parents or guardians who choose not to come to conferences don't care about their children's learning. There are all sorts of reasons why parents or guardians may choose not to attend a conference. Some may not feel comfortable in school, based on their own experiences as students. Some may have insurmountable schedule conflicts. You may never know the reasons some parents don't come. Luckily, it's not your job to judge. Rather, you may choose to offer another kind of communication (e.g., an email or a phone call) if you are able.

FOR FURTHER READING

Austin, T. (1994). *Changing the view: Student-led parent conferences.* Heinemann.

Bailey, J. M., & Guskey, T. R. (2001). *Implementing student-led conferences.* Corwin.

Berger, R. (2014). When students lead their learning. *Educational Leadership 71*(6). https://www.ascd.org/el/articles/when-students-lead-their-learning

McKibben, S. (2016). Parent-teacher conferences: Outdated or underutilized? *Education Update, 58*(9). https://www.ascd.org/el/articles/parent-teacher-conferences-outdated-or-underutilized

New Zealand Ministry of Education. (n.d.). *Student-led conferences and three-way conferences.* https://assessment.tki.org.nz/Reporting-to-parents-whanau/Examples-and-templates/Student-self-assessment-and-reflection/Student-led-conferences-and-three-way-conferences

Power, B. M., & Chandler, K. (1998). *Well-chosen words: Narrative assessments and report card comments.* Stenhouse.

20

Thinking in Terms of Assessment Systems

What Is an Assessment System?

An assessment system is an interconnected network of assessments that work together to serve the assessment information and use needs of multiple users for multiple purposes. Assessments at multiple levels are in play in every school district and may include classroom formative assessment, classroom summative assessment (grading), common formative assessment and interim/benchmark assessment, and state accountability testing. Figure 20.1 illustrates how assessments vary in purpose and focus.

Sometimes, other graphics are used to describe district assessment systems. Some authors, including Chappuis and colleagues (2021), envision a triangle with levels of assessment, with the classroom on the bottom and state accountability assessment at the top. Others, including Wiliam and colleagues (2019), envision similar assessment system components arranged in a chart. Any of these graphics can be helpful. Using the four quadrants envisioned in Figure 20.1 allows us to disentangle assessment purpose (formative/summative) from whether assessment is classroom-based or large-scale. By "classroom-based," we mean situated in the classroom as part of classroom learning, because even state accountability assessments are often taken in classrooms.

FIGURE 20.1
**Four-Quadrant Framework for Describing Types
of Assessments in an Assessment System**

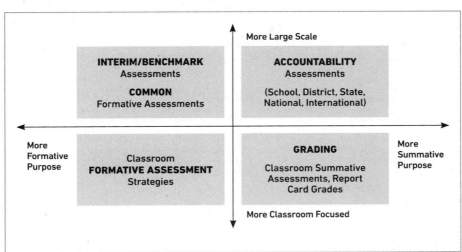

Source: From *How to Make Decisions with Different Kinds of Student Assessment Data* (p. 6), by S. M. Brookhart, 2016, ASCD. Copyright 2016 by ASCD.

Why Is It Important to Think in Terms of an Assessment System?

Ideally, these assessments should work together as a system, assessing student achievement of intended learning goals at different grain sizes and for different audiences, but maintaining a coherent conception of what is to be learned and what it means to do that. Decisions at all levels of the district, from immediate next steps in classroom learning to long-term strategic planning, will be optimal only if they are based on sound information.

How Do I Use an Assessment System in My Teaching and Assessment?

Whatever graphic organizer you prefer, an assessment system is not just a categorized list of all the assessments in use in a school district. For assessments to function as a system, they need to be working together in several ways. A well-functioning assessment system is

- **Comprehensive:** All valued learning outcomes are assessed by a range of assessment methods.

- **Balanced:** Sufficient meaningful, relevant information is provided to information users at all levels (e.g., administrators, teachers, parents/guardians, students) in a form (e.g., quantitative, qualitative, aggregated, individual) appropriate to the use.
- **Coherent:** The learning outcomes being assessed are consistent at all levels, that is, achievement standards are defined and assessed in similar ways in both classroom and large-scale assessments and in formative and summative assessments.
- **Continuous:** The system produces a stream of evidence over time, making possible tracking of both individuals and groups (e.g., classes, schools).

Purposes of Assessment

The horizontal axis in Figure 20.1 distinguishes assessments whose primary purpose is formative (to support and improve learning) from those whose primary purpose is summative (to summarize and report on learning). Of course, the boundaries are not hard and fast, as some assessments end up serving dual purposes, but the horizontal axis is still helpful for considering and using the assessment information.

Assessments on the left side (more formative purpose) are typically not graded, because they serve a "monitor and adjust" purpose aimed at improving learning while it is still happening. Chapters 1 through 7 present information about classroom formative assessment. Interim or benchmark assessments are assessments administered several times during the school year to track student learning or growth. Although they may be used for predictive (of the state accountability test), evaluative (of materials or programs), or instructional purposes, most often they are intended to at least inform instruction, a formative purpose. Interim assessments can also be sold as item banks from which districts construct their own assessments.

Assessments on the right side (more summative purpose) are typically used for reporting final achievement, at least as "final" as information gets in an educational system, where one can argue that learning continues from when students enter the system until when they leave it, and beyond, so that any assessment information is provisional, ready to be eclipsed by whatever comes next. Grades report final achievement for classroom learning, and accountability tests report final achievement for schools and districts.

Proximity to Classroom Learning

The vertical axis in Figure 20.1 distinguishes assessments whose primary reference is to individual student learning in the classroom from assessments whose primary reference is to the performance of groups of students. Assessments below the axis (more classroom-based) are typically within classroom measures. Classroom formative assessment helps individual students as they pursue learning targets in the classroom, for example, helping them decide where they need to spend more time or ask for help and what they understand pretty clearly. Classroom formative assessment helps teachers make decisions about immediate feedback to students and about next instructional moves. Classroom summative assessment (grading) helps students and teachers take stock of where they are at designated points in time, like the end of a unit or series of lessons, or the end of a report period. These assessments are primarily treated student-by-student, in an individual manner, and are not aggregated across students. The information from classroom level assessment is usually used by and for the learning of the same students who took the assessments.

Assessments above the axis (more large-scale) are typically of more use for administrative decisions or for longer-term instructional planning. Assessment results used for administrative purposes typically are aggregated, for example, reported as distributions or averages of performance for a class, grade, or school. Results can also be disaggregated, reporting distributions or averages for demographic or other sub-groups of students within a class, grade, or school, but these are also group measures. The results of these assessments sometimes support decisions for other students than the ones who took the assessment, for example, next year's students.

Learning Goals

A system of different assessments and uses is based on the learning goals that underlie the curriculum, both the written curriculum and the taught curriculum. In many districts, these learning goals are stated as standards, sometimes with performance expectations. Some independent schools have their own curricular goals that may or may not be based on standards. However formulated, learning goals are the mechanism for assuring an assessment system is comprehensive and coherent. Thus, the first bastion for an assessment system is the quality of the learning goals on which it is based.

Assuming high-quality learning goals, an assessment system is comprehensive if somewhere in the system, all valued learning goals are measured. The way they are measured will differ depending on the assessment's place in the system (Figure 20.1). Classroom formative assessment typically assesses small chunks of learning, for example, what students have learned in one lesson or a short sequence of lessons. So, for example, formative assessment might involve students' self-assessment of their ability to put commas in compound sentences. Classroom summative assessment typically assesses the larger—but still not too big—chunks of learning that form a unit of instruction, such as students' final achievement at the end of a unit on punctuation. Interim assessment, and to an even greater extent accountability assessment, typically assesses learning goals at a larger grain size (e.g., "writing conventions" or even just "language arts").

The key to comprehensiveness is that the learning goals are assessed throughout the system, in the grain sizes needed for the respective decisions to be made. Students and teachers need to know whether more review of commas in compound sentences is in order, while an administrator doesn't. However, the administrator does need to know whether, if one new position is available, it might be wiser to hire an ELA teacher or a math teacher.

The key to coherence is whether these learning goals are conceptualized in the same way throughout the system. For example, years ago in a state I was working in, the state accountability test in math was changed so that students not only had to solve problems but also show their work and explain their reasoning. This was in accordance with the new math standards the state had adopted. Some math teachers in that state had to rethink their classroom assessments, which had been more focused on doing a problem and getting the right answer than reasoning with mathematics or explaining the models they used in their problem solution. If classroom level assessment defines a learning goal one way and large-scale assessment defines it in another, students are caught in the middle, and the usefulness of the assessment information at both levels is compromised.

Users and Uses

Balanced assessment systems produce all the information various users need, and not information they don't need. We've already mentioned levels of users and noted that the decisions administrators need to make typically require aggregated information about fairly broad learning goals, while the decisions students and teachers need to make typically require individual information about small chunks of learning. A system that is balanced produces both. That doesn't mean that it produces equal amounts of information for all stakeholders at all levels. The nature of instruction and learning is such that more formative assessment information is needed than summative assessment, and more classroom-level information is needed than large-scale, aggregated information.

The unequal information needs make sense if you think about the decisions that are made on the basis of information about student achievement.

During each classroom lesson, teachers and students make literally hundreds of decisions. Some of them are very small, but each contributes to the ongoing learning, and each needs to be based on high-quality information. In contrast, administrative decisions tend to be larger in scope but less frequent—although they still need to be based on high-quality information.

Quality of Information

As this chapter has shown, an effective assessment system is a collection of individual assessments that together provide comprehensive, balanced, coherent, and continuous information about student learning. The whole is more than the sum of its parts. However, each individual assessment must do its part, and that means that the information from each individual assessment must be high-quality information. The quality of quantitative assessment information (e.g., numerical scores or categorical scales like grades) is typically evaluated by considering its *validity* and *reliability*. More generally for any assessment information, including qualitative information (e.g., observations or extended feedback), the credibility and trustworthiness of information is important.

Validity and reliability. Validity is a characteristic of score meaning. A measure is valid if the score means what it was intended to mean and is appropriate for its intended use. Reliability is also a characteristic of score meaning. A measure is reliable if it remains consistent across factors that should not matter (e.g., what time a test is given).

Consider a simple example. If a test is intended to measure students' ability to multiply fractions, then it should be the case that students who are accomplished at multiplying fractions do well and students who aren't do poorly. It shouldn't be the case, for example, that students who are good readers do better because the test contains a lot of wordy problems, so that some students who are accomplished at multiplying fractions but not at reading do poorly and would be deemed, by this test, as poor at multiplying fractions. Valid uses of the test scores might be to help decide on further instruction, for example, reviewing multiplication of fractions or moving on to dividing fractions. If the test scores don't function in this way—which can be checked—then the test is not a valid measure of multiplying fractions, no matter what the problems look like.

And none of this (measuring ability at multiplying fractions and using this information for instructional decisions) would be possible if the test scores weren't reliable. Students who are accomplished at multiplying fractions should score well no matter when they take the test, or which particular form (if, e.g., there is a Form A and Form B to discourage cheating) they take, and so on. There are other ways for a test to be unreliable, but these two examples will suffice for illustration here. If a test is unreliable, you can't have confidence in the results. Think of an old-fashioned spring scale. When the springs get old and worn, a person can get different weight readings by standing on the scale in different ways. That produces unreliable information. If you're using the scale to track the progress of your diet and your weight decreased by a pound, you would not know whether you'd lost a pound or the scale just weighed you a pound low that day. That scale wouldn't be very useful for helping you diet.

Credibility and trustworthiness. The principle that assessment information should be valid, or sound, applies for all kinds of information. The previous section described collecting information to establish reliability and validity for quantitative information. For qualitative information, like observations of student work or teacher recommendations, the same principle applies; you should be able to be confident that the information is credible and trustworthy. For example, you can check for bias in observations or bias in students' responses. Sometimes teachers overestimate the capabilities of their own students because they "just know he knows it," providing more positive observations than they would for similar work from a student who was not in their class. Or, for another example, sometimes students don't feel able to be honest in conversations about their work because they are afraid they will look "dumb," and so they try to cover up misunderstandings or gaps in understanding. High-quality qualitative information is as free from bias and other sources of misdirection as possible.

Assessment Audits

An assessment audit can be a helpful way to systematically organize information about assessments within a district and to check that the district assessments together form a system that is comprehensive, balanced, coherent, and continuous. Examples of protocols for an assessment audit are available (see, e.g., Chappuis et al., 2021, pp. 21–26). Local involvement is key; an external consultant can help, but only local educators can reflect on the uses made of various assessment information and whether that information is coherent throughout the system. A successful assessment audit may lead to the realization that some standards are assessed too often and may need to be removed or that some standards are not assessed, so assessment needs to be added. Importantly, a thorough assessment audit may reveal that standards are not assessed in a coherent manner throughout the system. For example, an assessment audit may reveal that what it means to think scientifically differs in different assessments, which causes a problem for interpreting results and ultimately for instruction.

How Do I Involve Students in an Assessment System?

In general, you can and should involve students as active participants in classroom-based assessment, both classroom formative assessment and grading, the two lower quadrants in Figure 20.1. If you think about it, it makes sense. Classroom formative assessment rests on learning targets and success criteria. A lesson has a learning target when students know what they are trying to learn and what they need to know and do to get there (see Chapter 2). If students are not aiming for a lesson's learning goal, then it isn't a target. Therefore, if students aren't involved, there isn't a learning target at all. When students use learning targets and success criteria, they not only reach learning goals, they also learn about the process of learning. Involving students in their learning promotes student self-regulation, meta-cognition, and self-efficacy.

Students can also be active participants in classroom grading (see Chapter 18). Formative assessment prepares students for their graded work (so there are "no surprises and no excuses," as Rick Stiggins [2017] likes to say). Students can also be involved in helping set classroom grading policies about deadlines, revisions and redo's, and so on. Negotiated and jointly monitored classroom policies give students some ownership of the process of monitoring and reporting their learning.

For more large-scale assessment, the two upper quadrants in Figure 20.1, the student's role is generally as a consumer, and the teacher's role is to communicate clearly to the student. Before a large-scale test, inform students of at least the following:

- What the test is and why it is being given
- When it will be given and under what conditions (e.g., paper or computer? timed?)
- What content it will cover and with what emphasis
- What format the test uses (e.g., multiple choice? constructed response?)
- How the test will be scored and reported

After the results are in, teachers may be called on to communicate to students about their performance and what it means for them and their learning.

What Are Some Common Misconceptions About Assessment Systems?

One common misconception is that an assessment system means simply that somewhere there is a list of all the assessments in use in a district. Assessments do not form a system unless the relationships between the various assessments are known; the assessments together provide comprehensive, balanced, coherent, and continuous information; and that assessment information at all levels is used appropriately to monitor and improve learning.

FOR FURTHER READING

Boudett, K. P., City, E. A., & Murnane, R. J. (2013). *Data wise: A step-by-step guide to using assessment results to improve teaching and learning* (Rev. ed.). Harvard Education Press.

Brookhart, S. M. (2016). *How to make decisions with different kinds of student assessment data.* ASCD.

Chappuis, S., Brookhart, S. M., & Chappuis, J. (2021). *Ten assessment literacy goals for school leaders.* Corwin.

Stiggins, R. (2017). *The perfect assessment system.* ASCD.

Strengthening Claims-based Interpretations and Uses of Local and Large-scale Science Assessment Scores Project (SCILLSS). (2017). *Ensuring rigor in local assessment systems: A self-evaluation protocol.* Nebraska Department of Education. https://www.scillsspartners.org/wp-content/uploads/2019/05/Local-Self-Evaluation-Protocol_FINAL_5-30-19.pdf

Wiliam, D., Brookhart, S., McTighe, J., & Stiggins, R. (2019). *Comprehensive and balanced assessment systems.* Learning Sciences International white paper #DW02-06. https://www.dylanwiliamcenter.com/wp-content/uploads/sites/3/2020/10/DW02-06-Assessment-Systems-WP-Digital.pdf

21

Interpreting Standardized Test Results

What Are Standardized Tests?

Standardized tests are intended to yield scores whose meaning is comparable across time and place. For example, the scores of a student who takes a standardized test in California on Monday should be comparable to the scores of a student who takes the same standardized test in Florida on Friday. To that end, the procedures for administration, materials, and scoring rules for a standardized test are the same no matter when or where it is given. This is very important for certain purposes, for example, for certain accountability tests or certain admission and placement tests.

Why Are Standardized Tests Important?

The classroom teacher's role in interpreting standardized test results is to understand, communicate to students and parents, and sometimes to use for decision making the results of tests that originated outside the classroom. The teacher is the first person a parent or guardian may call with questions about their child's test results.

How Do I Use Standardized Tests in My Teaching and Assessment?

Teachers can use the results of some standardized tests (e.g., some interim assessments) as one of several data points for decisions about instruction for individual students or groups of students. Considering additional information from student classroom work increases the soundness of instructional decisions based on interim assessments.

Other standardized tests, such as most state accountability assessments, are best used to raise general questions about students' group performance that can then be answered by investigating further. For example, low overall English language arts performance in a school might lead to the question "Why are our students not doing as well in ELA as we would like?" That question could then be investigated by teams that include ELA teachers and building administrators, looking at teaching practices, teaching materials, and student classroom work.

In any case, using information from standardized tests for instructional decisions, or even for simply explaining results to students and parents, requires a sound understanding of standardized test results. The following sections are a primer for interpreting standardized test results. First, we explain that different interpretations are made depending on whether a student's performance is compared to the performance of other students or to an external criterion. For each, we define some common types of scores and illustrate their meaning. Second, we discuss two concepts that are important to using scores for decision making: aggregation of scores and interpreting growth. Third, we discuss dashboards, graphics, and other aids to interpretation. This brief chapter can't cover everything about standardized tests, but these three basic sections will go a long way toward helping you think clearly about standardized test scores. Readers who want more information should consult the Further Reading list.

Referencing Frameworks, Common Types of Scores, and Their Meaning

A score by itself doesn't mean much. Say you got a score of 32 on a test. Thirty-two what? What does that mean? Further, suppose you knew that there were 40 one-point questions, and you got 32 correct. What does that mean? What were the questions about? Were they difficult or easy? To infer meaning from a score, you need a referencing framework. Scores can be compared to the scores of others, which is called norm-referencing; or they can be compared to preset criteria, which is called criterion-referencing. Recently, a hybrid referencing framework that uses a standard-setting process, typically drawing on both norm- and criterion-referencing methods, has been used to link scores to state achievement standards. Figure 21.1 gives some examples of common kinds of scores used in each referencing framework and how to interpret them.

FIGURE 21.1
Referencing Schemes and Associated Scores

Norm-referencing interprets a student's performance on an assessment by comparing it with the performance of other students.

- A *scale score* or *standard score* transforms a student's raw score on an assessment by placing it on an arbitrary scale using one of many available scaling methods.
- A *percentile rank* tells what percentage of students in a norm group scored below a student's score on an assessment.

Criterion-referencing interprets a student's performance on an assessment by comparing it with defined standards.

- *Percent correct* identifies the percentage of points a student scored on an assessment, which can be interpreted as a criterion-referenced score if the total possible points define a meaningful domain of learning.
- The *quality level* of a student's performance can be rated by using a rubric, rating scale, or checklist.
- The *speed* of a performance tells how quickly the student completes a task or how many tasks the student does in a certain amount of time (e.g., a keyboarding speed of 53 words per minute).
- The *precision* of a student's performance tells how accurate the student is at completing a task (e.g., a keyboarding accuracy of 92 percent or 8 errors in 100 words).

Standards-referencing interprets a student's performance on an assessment by comparing it with defined levels of proficiency typically set by using both norm- and criterion-referenced methods. The levels may be described using *achievement level descriptors*.

- *Proficiency levels* are typically identified for standards-based accountability assessments. For example, a student may score at Level 3 on the Smarter Balanced 5th grade English Language Arts and Literacy test.

Norm-referencing. Norm-referencing compares a student's score to the scores of other students in a norm group. Norm-referencing has been used longer than criterion- or standards-referencing. Traditional standardized tests like the Iowa Tests of Basic Skills are a good example. Norm-referencing does not tell you *what* you know, but whether you know more or less of it than others.

When interpreting norm-referenced scores, pay attention to the norm group. Returning to our example score of 32, what would you think if I told you your 32 was the highest score in the group? Before you celebrate, you should ask who was in the group. You would interpret that information differently if the norm group was composed of 1st graders than you would if the norm group was composed of college seniors.

The representativeness of the norm group for the purposes you want to use the scores for is a big issue. A standardized test should come with information about who was in the norm group. Interpret norm-referenced scores accordingly. Was the norm group composed of a representative sample of schools in the nation, taking into account both geographic location and socioeconomic status? Was attention paid to representing gender and ethnicity in the norm group? Did the norm group include students with special needs? Are data from the norm group recent, or are the norming data from years ago? Was the norm group just the local school district? Students can have several different norm-referenced scores, depending on the group used for comparison. For example, a student might be at the 50th percentile (half of the norm group scored higher, half scored lower) in terms of national norms but in the 30th percentile in local district norms.

Norm-referenced comparisons often, but not always, begin with the calculation of some type of *scale score,* sometimes called a standard score. These can be calculated in several different ways, typically by calculating a standard score (and there are several types of those, too) or by using one of several item response theory algorithms. The main point for you to understand here is that scale scores are on an arbitrary scale, not the intuitive "zero through the total possible points" scale you may be envisioning. Although this may sound complicated, the calculations that create a scale score actually add meaning to the scores. Instead of a mathematical explanation for that, try this thought experiment. What if you and someone else each got 32 questions out of 40 correct, but you got more of the harder questions correct? Saying you both got 32 slightly misrepresents your relative knowledge of whatever the test measured. This is not the only justification for using scaling methods to score standardized tests, just one of the simple ones that I hope convinces you that scaling can be useful.

Many standardized test results include the scale score. They also should tell you what the confidence interval (sometimes called the error band) around that score is. Because no test score is perfectly reliable, the confidence interval helps you interpret the margin of error, a concept you may be familiar with from political polling. For example, a student may have a scale score of 230 on a test, with a confidence interval between 225 and 235. That means 230 is the test's best estimate of the student's performance, and their true performance is very likely between 225 and 235.

But what does the scale score mean? We've already said the scale is arbitrary. The most common way people make sense of scale scores is to report the corresponding *percentile rank.* Don't confuse percentile ranks with percent correct, which is another kind of score altogether. A percentile rank tells the percentage of people in the norm group who scored lower than a particular score. Percentile ranks range from 1 to 99. For example, a student who scored at the 75th percentile on a test did better than three quarters of the students in the norm group. Sometimes, a related score called a *stanine* is reported, although its use is declining. Stanines report where a student's score falls on a normal distribution divided into nine parts. Stanines range from 1 to 9, and the idea was that fewer categories would eliminate the risk of over-interpretation that comes with percentile ranks that have 99 categories.

My advice for norm-referenced scores is to focus on percentile ranks and interpret them in light of the size of the confidence interval and the composition of the norm group. And as always, whether interpreting norm-referenced scores or any other assessment results, never use just one measure for an important decision. Instead, use multiple measures and interpret what the set of results is telling you.

Criterion-referencing. Criterion-referencing compares a student's score to defined requirements. For example, a person may be able to keyboard 50 words per minute, or correctly punctuate compound sentences at the 80 percent level, or write an essay that scores a 5 on the Ideas criterion of the 6-point 6+1 Trait Writing Rubrics (Education Northwest, 2021), meaning "Presents a clear, focused, and substantive main idea with convincing development."

The most common criterion-referenced scores are percentages, quality level, speed, or precision. Some standardized tests, for example, use norm-referenced scores for overall test scores and then report student percentage correct on items representing individual skills. Quality levels are typically judged using a rubric and are often used for writing assessment. Speed (e.g., keyboarding 50 words per minute) and precision (e.g., measures accurately to the nearest half inch) are also criterion-referenced scores.

Criterion-referenced scores do not take into account the performance of others. For example, every essay in the class could have been at a level 5 or 6 on the Ideas criterion of the writing rubrics. Or maybe not—criterion-referenced scores do not tell you that information. My advice for criterion-referenced scores is to interpret the information as the best estimate of a student's performance against the requirements, keeping in mind, as for any assessment, that the score is an estimate of true performance subject to measurement error and that more than one measure should be used for major decisions.

Standards-referencing. With the advent of the standards movement came the need to reference students' performance against defined levels on a standard, or, in the case of state accountability assessments, sometimes all the standards in a content area (e.g., ELA, math). Sometimes there are only two levels (e.g., mastery, non-mastery), and sometimes there are more, typically three to five. For example, the Smarter Balanced summative assessment reports scores on four levels for mathematics and English language arts/literacy. The descriptions of those defined levels typically are called achievement level descriptors or performance level descriptions.

Placing students into standards-referenced achievement levels most commonly involves calculating scale scores—as we have seen, a norm-referenced process—and then conducting one or a series of standard-setting studies with expert panels (including teachers, typically) to set cut points on the scale to define categories of performance that match the achievement level descriptors, which is a criterion-referenced process. Standards-referenced scores, then, are a kind of hybrid of norm- and criterion-referencing. For an example see the Smarter Balanced (2022) explanation of their standards-referencing process in the Further Reading section.

Also note that standards-referenced scores calculated in this way are subject to two different sources of error: the measurement error in a scale score, discussed above, and the error associated with the panel judgments. This is not cause to dismiss standards-referenced results—they are still the best estimate we have of student performance on that kind of test—just one more reason to seek out additional evidence before making important decisions.

Another way to classify students into levels is to use diagnostic classification modeling, which uses students' performance on an assessment to calculate their probability of mastery or non-mastery for each level assessed. Mastery determinations on individual levels are aggregated up to produce overall summative mastery classifications for standards. For an example, see the Dynamic Learning Maps (2022) description of their process in the Further Reading section.

Standards-referenced scores created with diagnostic classification modeling are probabilistic scores, which means that each reported assessment level is the most likely level of student achievement, given their performance on the test. Again, this is not cause to dismiss the results. An assessment literate teacher simply knows that these scores are estimates—typically good ones—but just estimates, and they should seek other supporting information for major decisions.

Interpreting Groups or Patterns of Scores

Whether norm-, criterion-, or standards-referenced, obtaining scores for individual students is typically not the only reason for administering a standardized test. For many purposes, such as school accountability, program evaluation, and many administrative decisions, standardized test scores are examined by group or over time, or both.

Aggregation and disaggregation. The *unit of analysis* is the unit a report describes. For an individual score report, the unit of analysis is the student. Standardized test results are often reported at the class, school, or district level, as well. Grouping scores is called *aggregation* and separating scores into smaller component groups is called *disaggregation*. For example, state accountability data is often disaggregated into groups based on demographics (e.g., gender, ethnicity, socioeconomic status), special needs status, or English learner status. The unit of analysis should be appropriate to the decisions you are looking to make.

Another thing to keep in mind with aggregated data is that one statistic, typically an average of some sort, is used to represent a group. Using aggregated measures of group performance trades being able to summarize a group with one statistic for the detail available in individual scores. In fact, the group will have a *distribution* (a spread) around that average. Whenever you use an aggregated score (e.g., a mean), look for a measure of spread around it (e.g., a standard deviation) so you can get a sense of how typical the aggregated score is.

Growth. Sometimes standardized test scores are examined over time to give a sense of growth, typically defined as change in performance over two or more time points. There are many different ways to do this, and they all provide different information. For example, if you want to examine the growth of students over time at your school, you need to look at the scores of the same students over time, for example, last year's 3rd grade scores and this year's 4th grade scores for the same students. But then, curriculum and instruction is not the same for each time point, and that may affect the change in performance. If you want to examine improvement in instruction over time, you could look at scores from the same grade from year to year, but then students are not the same and that may affect the change in performance.

Sometimes, *growth models* are calculated using standardized test scores. A growth model is "a collection of definitions, calculations, or rules that summarizes student performance over two or more time points" (Castellano & Ho, 2013, p. 16). There are many different growth models; Castellano and Ho describe seven of them and explain the interpretations each can support (or not support). Some growth models seek to estimate the amount of growth using various statistics, some seek to predict future performance, and some seek to explain what caused the growth. The latter have been called "value added" models. As attractive as this may sound, the parameters associated with value added models have been found to be unreliable, limiting their use.

If you need to work with growth or growth models, our recommendation is that you understand what model you are using and what primary interpretations it supports. Then, use the results appropriately. For example, if you are looking at the simple gains in scores for a particular class, from the end of the previous school year to the end of the current year, you may be disappointed if that class shows very little gain. However, you don't have any information that the teacher was the cause of that disappointing result, or that the instructional materials, or the students, or anything else was the cause.

Aids to Interpretation

Score reports from standardized tests are changing rapidly. Traditional paper score reports, typically issued for individuals, classes, and schools, relied on the assessment literacy of the reader for interpretation. In addition, they were static reports that informed the reader of test results at one point in time. Sometimes, as is also the case today, the test publisher would also publish interpretive guides.

Score reporting is also changing. Even static score reports often use informational graphics (e.g., red/yellow/green colors, number lines, charts) to make interpretation more intuitive. Sometimes they include links to recommended remediation or study materials.

Dashboards and other interactive score reporting tools can summarize more information than just the scores from one test. Sometimes dashboards allow the viewer to perform analyses, as well. For example, a teacher might be able to pull up individual student records from a dashboard and sort and arrange them in various ways. Some large-scale tests, such as NAEP or PISA, have data explorer tools where you can run various analyses and build custom reports yourself.

Whatever the form of standardized test results, whether it's a static document or an interactive dashboard, I recommend you first identify what information is given (e.g., who was assessed, what was assessed, scale scores, percentiles, proficiency levels, and so on) to make sure you know what each element of the report is. Once you have done that, interpret the scores, mindful of the referencing framework used and the amount of error in the scores. If you have questions, seek information from an interpretive guide, if there is one, or from a colleague with some educational measurement training, for example, a school psychologist.

How Do I Involve Students in Standardized Tests?

The teacher's main responsibility for involving students in standardized testing is to prepare them for testing. Before a standardized test, students should know that they will be assessed, why they will be assessed, what the assessment will cover, and how their results will be used. You can also make sure your students are familiar with the format of the test, for example, how to make a selection for a multiple-choice question, or how to write a direct response to a short-answer question. You don't need to go overboard here—I have seen some "test prep" happening in classes that had students doing nothing but multiple-choice questions for weeks before a state test. This kind of obsessive practice limits learning. One place where format familiarity is of particular interest currently is with tests administered on computers, which sometimes use nontraditional item types. For example, students may be asked to slide a bar from left to right to simulate the movement of the sun over some crops in an interactive item. Students who take tests on computers should be familiar enough with computers to perform simple tasks like this without interfering with their test performance.

What Are Some Common Misconceptions About Standardized Tests?

One common misconception is that standardized tests are necessarily multiple-choice tests. This is not true. Many standardized tests do use multiple-choice questions, but almost any assessment can be standardized. Many states administer standardized writing assessments, for example. Other types of performance assessment can be standardized, as well.

Less of a misconception and more of an overgeneralization, some people think that all standardized tests are bad, or stifle student creativity, or something like that. In fact, standardized tests are very good for a specific purpose, namely, any time you want to be able to compare students' scores in a valid manner across time or place. The problem comes when standardized tests are overused or overinterpreted, for example, when they are used to the exclusion of classroom assessment or other relevant information for placing students in school programs. Another example of overinterpreting the importance of standardized test scores is using them as the sole measure of teacher effectiveness, when teacher effectiveness also entails many other factors.

FOR FURTHER READING

Boudett, K. P., City, E. A., & Murnane, R. J. (2013). *Data wise: A step-by-step guide to using assessment results to improve teaching and learning* (Rev. ed.). Harvard Education Press.

Brookhart, S. M. (2016). *How to make decisions with different kinds of student assessment data.* ASCD.

Castellano, K. E., & Ho, A. D. (2013). *A practitioner's guide to growth models.* Council of Chief State School Officers. https://scholar.harvard.edu/files/andrewho/files/a_pracitioners_guide_to_growth_models.pdf

Dynamic Learning Maps. (2022). *Assessment results.* https://dynamiclearningmaps.org/assessment-results

Education Northwest. (2021). *6+1 trait writing rubrics: Grades 3–12.* https://educationnorthwest.org/sites/default/files/resources/traits-rubrics-3-12.pdf

Mertler, C. A. (2007). *Interpreting standardized test scores: Strategies for data-driven instructional decision making.* Sage.

Smarter Balanced. (2022). *Reporting scores.* https://validity.smarterbalanced.org/scoring/

Index

The letter *f* following a page locator denotes a figure.

About the Author

 **Susan M. Brookhart, PhD,** is professor emerita in the School of Education at Duquesne University and an independent educational consultant and author based in Los Angeles, California. She was the 2007–2009 editor of *Educational Measurement: Issues and Practice* and is currently an associate editor of *Applied Measurement in Education.* She is the author or coauthor of numerous books, articles, and book chapters on classroom assessment, teacher professional development, and evaluation. She has been named the 2014 Jason Millman Scholar by the Consortium for Research on Educational Assessment and Teaching Effectiveness (CREATE) and is the recipient of the 2015 Samuel J. Messick Memorial Lecture Award from ETS/TOEFL. Brookhart's research interests include the role of both formative and summative classroom assessment in student motivation and achievement, the connection between classroom assessment and large-scale assessment, and grading.

Brookhart also works with schools, districts, regional educational service units, universities, and states doing professional development. She received her PhD in educational research and evaluation from The Ohio State University, after teaching in both elementary and middle schools. She can be reached at suebrookhart@gmail.com.

Related ASCD Resources: Assessment

At the time of publication, the following resources were available (ASCD stock numbers in parentheses).

Assessing with Respect: Everyday Practices That Meet Students' Social and Emotional Needs by Starr Sackstein (#121023)

Assessment Literacy for Educators in a Hurry by W. James Popham (#119009)

Changing the Grade: A Step-by-Step Guide to Grading for Student Growth by Jonathan Cornue (#118029)

Charting a Course to Standards-Based Grading: What to Stop, What to Start, and Why It Matters by Tim R. Westerberg (#117010)

Checking for Understanding: Formative Assessment Techniques for Your Classroom, 2nd Edition, by Douglas Fisher and Nancy Frey (#115011)

Demonstrating Student Mastery with Digital Badges and Portfolios by David Niguidula (#119026)

Fast and Effective Assessment: How to Reduce Your Workload and Improve Student Learning by Glen Pearsall (#118002)

Giving Students a Say: Smarter Assessment Practices to Empower and Engage by Myron Dueck (#119013)

How to Create and Use Rubrics for Formative Assessment and Grading by Susan M. Brookhart (#112001)

How to Design Questions and Tasks to Assess Student Thinking by Susan M. Brookhart (#114014)

How to Give Effective Feedback to Your Students, 2nd Edition, by Susan M. Brookhart (#116066)

How to Look at Student Work to Uncover Student Thinking by Susan M. Brookhart and Alice Oakley (#122011)

How to Make Decisions with Different Kinds of Student Assessment Data by Susan M. Brookhart (#116003)

How to Use Grading to Improve Learning by Susan M. Brookhart (#117074)

Learning Targets: Helping Students Aim for Understanding in Today's Lesson by Connie M. Moss and Susan M. Brookhart (#112002)

Mastering Formative Assessment Moves: 7 High-Leverage Practices to Advance Student Learning by Brent Duckor and Carrie Holmberg (#116011)

Peer Feedback in the Classroom: Empowering Students to Be the Experts by Starr Sackstein (#117020)

The Perfect Assessment System by Rick Stiggins (#117079)

Questioning for Formative Feedback: Meaningful Dialogue to Improve Learning by Jackie Acree Walsh (#119006)

Rethinking Homework: Best Practices That Support Diverse Needs, 2nd Edition, by Cathy Vatterott (#119001)

Student-Led Assessment: Promoting Agency and Achievement Through Portfolios and Conferences by Starr Sackstein (#123033)

For up-to-date information about ASCD resources, go to www.ascd.org. You can search the complete archives of *Educational Leadership* at www.ascd.org/el. To contact us, send an email to member@ascd.org or call 1-800-933-2723 or 703-578-9600.

WHOLE CHILD
TENETS

1 **HEALTHY**
Each student enters school healthy and learns about and practices a healthy lifestyle.

2 **SAFE**
Each student learns in an environment that is physically and emotionally safe for students and adults.

3 **ENGAGED**
Each student is actively engaged in learning and is connected to the school and broader community.

4 **SUPPORTED**
Each student has access to personalized learning and is supported by qualified, caring adults.

5 **CHALLENGED**
Each student is challenged academically and prepared for success in college or further study and for employment and participation in a global environment.

ascd whole child

The ASCD Whole Child approach is an effort to transition from a focus on narrowly defined academic achievement to one that promotes the long-term development and success of all children. Through this approach, ASCD supports educators, families, community members, and policymakers as they move from a vision about educating the whole child to sustainable, collaborative actions.

Classroom Assessment Essentials relates to the **supported** and **challenged** tenets.

For more about the ASCD Whole Child approach, visit **www.ascd.org/wholechild.**

Become an ASCD member today!
Go to www.ascd.org/joinascd
or call toll-free: 800-933-ASCD (2723)